# GREENING YOUR COMMUNITY

## Strategies for Engaged Citizens

## Jill Doucette
### with Mark Boysen

**Self-Counsel Press**
*(a division of)*
International Self-Counsel Press Ltd.
USA    Canada

Self-Counsel Press acknowledges the financial support of the Government of Canada through the Canada Book Fund for our publishing activities.

Printed in Canada.

First edition: 2015

**Library and Archives Canada Cataloguing in Publication**

Doucette, Jill, 1986-, author
    Greening your community : strategies for engaged citizens / Jill Doucette.

(Self-Counsel green series)
Issued in print and electronic formats.
ISBN 978-1-77040-223-2 (pbk.).—ISBN 978-1-77040-982-8 (epub).—ISBN 978-1-77040-983-5 (kindle)

    1. Community development--Environmental aspects. 2. Sustainable living. 3. Community life--Environmental aspects. 4. Sustainable development. I. Title. II. Series: Self-Counsel green series

HN49.C6D69 2015        307.1'4        C2014-908245-2
                                      C2014-908246-0

Icons at the beginning of each chapter are provided by Travis Doucette and used with permission.

Chapter 10 interview quotes from Eric Bonham, used with permission.

**Self-Counsel Press**
(a division of)
International Self-Counsel Press Ltd.

Bellingham, WA                    North Vancouver, BC
USA                               Canada

# Contents

**Introduction**                                                    xi

**1  Rethinking Our Communities:
    People, Planet, Prosperity**                                    1

   1.  How Others Interpret a Green Community          3

**2  Taking Action**                                                6

   1.  Starting Small                                   7

   2.  Mobilize Change                                  7

   3.  Outreach Tools                                  11

**3  Food Security**                                               13

   1.  Growing Food Locally                            14

   2.  The Environmental Impact of Meat                15

   3.  The Environmental Impact of Seafood             16

   4.  Food Waste                                      19

   5.  Community Gardening                             21

      5.1  Guerilla gardening            22

|  | 5.2 | Sharing backyards | 23 |
| 6. | | Urban Agriculture | 24 |
| 7. | | Urban Livestock | 24 |
| 8. | | Farming Food Instead of Manicuring Lawns | 26 |
| 9. | | Stop Using Pesticides | 27 |

## 4 Green Events — 29

| 1. | | Community Events | 30 |
| 2. | | Family Events | 31 |
| 3. | | Zero-Trash Events | 34 |
| 4. | | Environmental Action Events | 36 |

## 5 Using Green Transportation — 40

| 1. | | The Cost of Vehicle Ownership | 41 |
| 2. | | Transportation Alternatives | 42 |
|  | 2.1 | Bicycling | 43 |
|  | 2.2 | Walking | 45 |
|  | 2.3 | Car- and bike-sharing programs | 46 |
| 3. | | Drive Greener | 46 |
|  | 3.1 | Electric vehicles | 47 |

## 6 Foundations of a Green Home — 49

| 1. | | Home Size and Location | 50 |
| 2. | | Evaluating Your Home | 52 |
|  | 2.1 | Heating your home | 54 |
|  | 2.2 | Electronics, appliances, and lights | 56 |
| 3. | | Living Green in an Apartment or Condo | 57 |
| 4. | | Daily Practices Make a Difference | 59 |

## 7 Water Systems — 60

| 1. | | Watershed Areas | 62 |
| 2. | | Water Use in Our Communities | 63 |
| 3. | | Reducing Water Pollution | 66 |
| 4. | | Reducing Water Use in Our Homes | 67 |

**8 Renewable Energy: Seeking the Net-Zero Community** 70

1. Why We Care about Climate Change 71
   1.1 Sea-level rise 71
   1.2 Increased forest fires 71
   1.3 Natural environment impacts 71
   1.4 Food impacts 72
   1.5 Water supply 72
2. Renewable Energy in Your Community 72
   2.1 Photovoltaic solar panels 73
   2.2 Solar hot water systems 74
   2.3 Geo-exchange systems 74
   2.4 Biomass or bioenergy 75
   2.5 Wind power 75
   2.6 Hydro power 76
3. Do-It-Yourself Solar Collector 76
4. Carbon Offsets 77
5. Purchasing Renewable Energy 79

**9 Recycling, Composting, and Trash** 80

1. Reduce, Reuse, Recycle 81
   1.1 Composting 83
   1.2 Plastics 84
   1.3 Batteries 84
   1.4 Styrofoam 85
   1.5 Mattresses 86
2. Set a Lofty Goal: Zero-Waste Work, School, and Home 86
3. Consumer-to-Consumer Selling and the Sharing Economy 87
4. Upcycling 88
5. Circular Economy 88

**10 Natural Environment and Green Spaces** 90

1. Integrating Nature into Our Communities 91
2. Preserving Natural Areas 94

**11 Arts and the Environmental Movement**    98

**12 The Green Economy and Entrepreneurship**    101

   1. Local Economy    102

   2. Green Business Practices    104

      2.1 Encourage the local business community to go green    106

   3. New, Green Businesses and Jobs    107

   3.1 Innovative business    109

**13 Sustainable Cities and Helping Yours Become One**    111

   1. Cities That Lead    112

      1.1 Vancouver    113

      1.2 San Francisco    113

      1.3 Portland    113

      1.4 Seattle    113

      1.5 Toronto    114

      1.6 New York    114

      1.7 International cities worth watching    114

   2. What Makes a Community a Green Leader?    115

      2.1 Green champions    115

   3. Working with City Hall    117

**14 Measure Success**    119

   1. Measuring at the Project Level    119

   2. Measuring at the City Level    121

**Checklist**

1 Planning Considerations for a Green Event    32

**Tables**

1 Aspects of Your Community    2

2 Determine the Barriers and Take Action    11

3 Examples of Green Business Programs and Criteria    107

4 Environmental Ventures    108

5 River Cleanup Project SMART Goals    120

6 Key Performance Indicators: Local Business Example    122

# *Notice to Readers*

Laws are constantly changing. Every effort is made to keep this publication as current as possible. However, the author, the publisher, and the vendor of this book make no representations or warranties regarding the outcome or the use to which the information in this book is put and are not assuming any liability for any claims, losses, or damages arising out of the use of this book. The reader should not rely on the author or the publisher of this book for any professional advice. Please be sure that you have the most recent edition.

**Note:** The fees quoted in this book are correct at the date of publication. However, fees are subject to change without notice. For current fees, please check with the court registry or appropriate government office nearest you.

Prices, commissions, fees, and other costs mentioned in the text or shown in samples in this book probably do not reflect real costs where you live. Inflation and other factors, including geography, can cause the costs you might encounter to be much higher or even much lower than those we show. The dollar amounts shown are simply intended as representative examples.

Website links often expire or web pages move, at the time of this book's publication the links were current.

# *Acknowledgments*

Thank you first to Kirk LaPointe and the Self-Counsel Press team for taking an interest in this topic and launching the *Green Series*. These books have shared innovative stories of how we can make a difference in how we work, live, and build our communities to create a better future for humanity and other species. Thanks also to those who have supported us through our caffeinated endeavor of writing this book between environmental projects, and after hours.

Personally, I would like to thank the environmental pioneers and thought-leaders that worked tirelessly in the decades before I did. David Suzuki, Paul Hawken, Amory Lovins, Nancy Turner, Mark Hume, James Rowe, Eric Bonham, and Monika Winn your work has inspired me and carved a path for a younger generation to explore ideas of how our communities can coexist symbiotically with nature. And to those of you who are turning these ideas into action, thank you for making it easy to find incredible stories of environmental leadership. Seeing the sheer volume of human action on the ground today has given me hope for a greener, more connected, and healthier future for humanity and the planet.

— Jill Doucette

Thank you to those who care to make their community a better place and don't receive, or seek, the credit for doing so.

— Mark Boysen

# Introduction: What Is a Green Community?

Around the world, there are various definitions for a "green community." Every community is different, and in its own way, it can promote sustainable living and enhance the quality of its natural environment. Green communities are those that balance the health of local citizens, the economy, and the environment. These are efficient, engaged, and innovative communities that are working to create solutions to environmental issues, while promoting social well-being and new economic opportunities. There is a growing awareness that where and how we live can have a dramatic impact on the planet and future generations.

Becoming a green community often raises questions about leadership. We can buy into the idea of social, economic, and environmental well-being, but who is going to lead the charge? Who sets the goals? Who organizes the action and sets the policies to get us there?

We need regulation and we also need action. It can seem an intangible journey for a single individual, whether the person is in the government, or not. I have grappled with this question of where leadership comes from and realized that it is different in every community.

In some, there is clearly leadership from the nonprofit organizations; sometimes it's the businesses, schools, counties, industry associations, local government, or small group of concerned citizens. But there is one common thread they share: The leadership comes from small groups bound together with a common sense of purpose and foreseeable outcome. They are connected by their passion for the cause and they commit to seeing it happen, and enjoy the process of making that change, knowing that their efforts have meaning.

These small groups gather, share, plan, and inspire one another towards their common goal and they bring their resources (i.e., time, money, knowledge) with them. Groups like this have accomplished incredible things that I could never imagine came from a dusty living room, local pub, or meeting room outside of office hours. Returning to the question, who should lead the path towards a greener community? Whoever shares a vision for what it could become.

The opportunities to green our communities lie in the hands of the individuals that are a part of these groups. Thus, this book is written for the engaged citizen. While different levels of government can support sustainability programs, it is up to the residents of communities to drive change forward.

It is up to each of us to do our part to transform where we live and create the communities of the future. Yes, greening requires everyone, from the local energy utility to parks staff and school teachers. However, in every community there are those that will seize an idea and take action. These individuals and groups inspire and mobilize their neighbors and peers, and become a part of the movement towards a greener community. This book is for you if you want to make a lasting impression on your community — and make the world a better place.

Within each chapter are action ideas, checklists, case studies, and planning tools for how to take action. It is loaded with recommendations for making meaningful change and rallying your community behind causes that matter on a local or global scale. Some of these ideas are simple and some are more complex, but all will contribute to a healthier planet and cohesive community. Laden with stories of audacity and courage of people around the world, *Greening Your Community* can provide you with new perspective and concrete ideas for how to make your community a better place to live.

The term "green" will appear often in this book. We recognize this is a subjective term, but it will spare you from reading "reduced environmental impact and improve human well-being" hundreds of times throughout these chapters. Arguably, "environmental," "eco-friendly," and "natural" are equally subjective. So, for the purposes of this book, we have chosen "green" and will define it here:

**Green:** Using an awareness of the importance of natural ecosystems to make a choice towards solutions that have reduced environmental impact and enhance human well-being.

We will also use the term "sustainability." For a definition, we will reference the *Brundtland Report*:

"**Sustainability:** The ability to meet the needs of the current generation without compromising future generations."

As Sustainable Seattle defines it:

"Sustainable is the long-term, cultural, economic and environmental health and vitality with the emphasis on long-term, together with the importance of linking our social, financial, and environmental well-being."

This book will address the various components of a green community. In each chapter, you will find examples of actions that you can do to help your community go green. The key is to get enough information so you can focus your effort, rally support behind your cause, and see results.

# 1
# *Rethinking Our Communities: People, Planet, Prosperity*

Where you live has a profound impact on your lifestyle and how you view the world. By definition, a community is "a group of people living in the same place or having a particular characteristic in common." It could also be defined as: "The people of a district or country considered collectively, especially in the context of social values and responsibilities." A community is both of these. It is a place that a group of people share as well as a shared connection — a cause, common interest, trait, or values that unites a group, making them more cohesive. A community is like a fingerprint: Each one is distinctly different, but similar patterns can be grouped into categories.

Dominating industries, cultures, and ecology are broad attributes that make up each community. Refined further, the political environment, languages, subcultures, climate, and topography shape the way our cities are built and how our community interacts. In every community, there are various interactions, motives, and considerations at play. It is not enough to look at your community through a profit-generation lens, or a social lens, or an environmental lens. Too often, single-minded groups end up alienating themselves from what could be a complementary cause because they fail to see the interrelatedness and how they could really work together. Social, environmental, and prosperity issues are inherently intertwined, which can make them very complex. To gain perspective, it is important to look at a community from a bird's-eye view and understand all of the forces and considerations at play. Look at it as a whole, rather than a collection of parts.

What are the aspects of your community that make up its "fingerprint"? Look at Table 1 as an example of the unique characteristics and how they interact to determine opportunities for engagement in sustainability. When you have an understanding of what you're looking for, you can create your own table to analyze the unique aspects of your community.

### Table 1
### Aspects of Your Community

| Social (People) | Environmental (Planet) | Economic (Prosperity) |
|---|---|---|
| *Example:*<br>• Language and heritage: English, French, Spanish.<br>• Artistic community.<br>• High percentage of retired population.<br>• Youth leave the city in search of better jobs. | *Example:*<br>• Rain forest ecology, with diverse habitats, shorelines, and estuaries..<br>• Issues of water pollution and deforestation.<br>• Opportunity to reuse waste and turn into new product. | *Example:*<br>• Unemployment rate is 6 percent, mostly youth.<br>• University, government, and tech sectors are the major employers.<br>• Tech sector is dominant, followed by tourism. |
| **Your Community:** | **Your Community:** | **Your Community:** |
| | | |
| | | |

You will notice that one of the aspects under the environmental category in Table 1, "Opportunity to reuse waste and turn it into a new product," overlaps with both the social and economic categories. Using waste and turning it into new product reduces the need for raw resource extraction which reduces pressures on natural ecosystems, but it can also create new revenue streams by producing new local products (economic) and generating jobs for the underemployed and youth that are leaving town (social). The artistic community could also thrive with this opportunity to be creative and find ways to reuse waste.

Look for those opportunities that have an array of benefits. In many cases, we can look to solve environmental problems while creating social well-being and economic prosperity, if we take the right approach and consider our community as a whole.

Ask yourself: Does your community work to balance the natural environment and facilitate the well-being of citizens? Could it be doing more in the following areas?

- **People:** What does a green community mean for the people who live within it? How does it affect global society?

- **Planet:** What does a green community mean for the other species, and the ecosystems? How much does the community take from the land and what does it give back?

- **Prosperity:** What does a green community mean for its economic engine? How does the community thrive and become more resilient?

## 1. How Others Interpret a Green Community

While there are many definitions of a green community, we took to the streets and asked people what a green community is to them. Here are some responses:

- "One that is full of life with growing plants, and people in the community."

- "I think of it as equal rights — people are working together, sharing, and being fair to one another."

- "It's really the best community possible. Everywhere you go there are blueberries, apples, and tomatoes. You can make a sandwich just by walking down the road!"

- "One that manages waste responsibly, and doesn't put profits before livelihoods and health benefits of the people living in it."

- "It is flourishing with plants, pollinators, birds, and fertile soil with active worms and microbes."

These answers touch on many different aspects of what can be considered a green community; some referenced a local economy, others talked of alternative energy and recycling, and even more discussed the sense of community and fairness. We found no wrong answers because all of these facets make up what could be a green community, but one response in particular captures the essence of this book: "It's really the best community possible." We believe the best community possible is one that keeps its people safe, protects its natural environment, finds ways to reduce the environmental impact from within the community, and sustains a local economy: That is a green community.

At first, it may seem idealistic, but there are communities emulating this today, and many more that are striving towards this notion of healthier, happy citizens, environmental sustainability, and profitable local economies. It is not impossible, and in fact, many cities are finding that one aspect influences the other. When addressed in tandem, environmental initiatives can have a positive impact of social factors, such as health, happiness, and new jobs. Likewise, social initiatives such as skills training and support for marginalized communities can have positive spin-offs for the local economy.

In contrast, a community on the opposite end of the spectrum, a "nongreen" community would be fraught with environmental issues, disconnected from the natural world:

- "One that has terrible traffic and generates huge amounts of waste."

- "It would probably smell and be smoggy. There would be health issues."

- "A city of just concrete and buildings lacking life and community spaces."

- "People not connected to the natural world, or each other."

- "I think of multilane roads, large landfills, resource extraction, and oversized homes."

This community doesn't sound pleasant at all.

While the journey and steps are different for every community, the common objectives of a green community are a healthy environment, the well-being of its citizens, and a strong local economy. You don't need to be an environmentalist, or a social worker, to understand the value of a green economy, it's something that benefits everyone, and the rest of the world. It's aiming to be the best possible community.

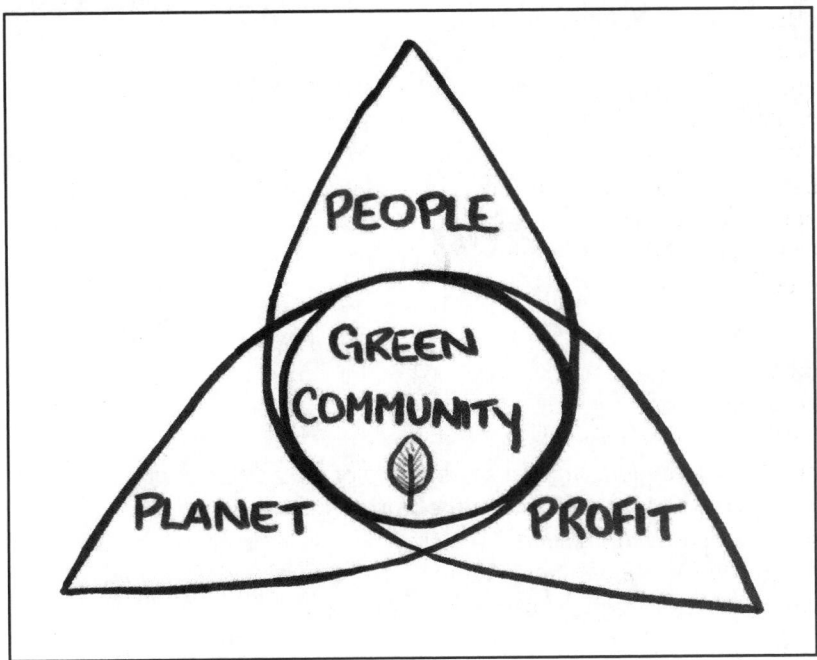

Diagram 1: Green Community: People, Planet, Profit

# 2
# Taking Action

> "Never doubt that a small group of thoughtful, committed people can change the world. Indeed, it is the only thing that ever has."

> — Margaret Mead

 Greening your community may seem daunting, or even impossible. How does one tackle an entire community, when every facet is woven in a thick web of complexity? Property ownership, regulations, and bureaucratic systems can be viewed as insurmountable walls of nonsense. In our minds, this can get tangled into an inconceivable mess. While it is easy to become overwhelmed, know that in each green community around the world, what makes it so fantastically progressive is the collective will of inspired, passionate individuals. These groups have been able to pool their capacities and, with small steps over time, create big change. In Portland, Austin, Vancouver, and Victoria, groups and ecstatic individuals are spearheading topics such as solar energy, bicycle commuting, local food, community arts, affordable housing, and green business sharing economy. Don't be afraid to start small and take action.

# 1. Starting Small

While I was in University, I became discouraged with the field I was studying and, like many young students, I felt lost. Looking to find something new, I decided to take some random electives. That included Astronomy, Spanish, Economics, and Environmental Studies. I always had an affinity for nature as a child, but when I learned about current environmental issues and solutions, it struck a chord. I wanted to get involved, but I had no idea how.

A guest speaker came to class and talked about a student-run organization called the University of Victoria Sustainability Project. Without any experience, I offered to help where needed. I started with putting up posters around campus about the organization's projects. They were starting an on-campus farmers' market, recycling for electronics, and setting up better composting. This modest volunteer role transformed my entire career direction, but it started very small.

Once I was involved, I learned from my peers — soaking up information like a sponge. I took on more duties and led a few initiatives. I was able to bring in my business background, finding ways to not only make a positive environmental difference, but an economical one as well. This led to involvement in the World Student Environmental Summit in Kyoto, Japan. From there, a small group of these students from Japan, Canada, and Germany, formed the World Student Environmental Network. This network continues today, hosting World Summits in countries around the world, and bringing students together from dozens of countries to talk about sustainability issues. Sometimes I look back at that class, and those posters. I could have never guessed that so much would snowball from so little.

# 2. Mobilize Change

When I learn of remarkable environmental projects, I always want to know how these ideas took root and turned into action. Looking at well-established projects today, it can be hard to imagine how they got started. Curious about the impetus for the project and the spark that made it happen; I ask these questions:

- What was the first course of action?

- Who took the lead?

- How did they get people on board?

- How did they share their idea?

Surprisingly, it is rare to hear that the project was government-led, or spearheaded by an industry with massive resources. What I hear is the same story, over and over again. It goes something like this: A small group of individuals were all ticked off about the same problem. Over a casual hangout they decided, "Let's stop talking about this and do something about it." That started a movement. They began meeting regularly, plotting their course, and pulling together others that shared their vision. After some planning and partnership development, they picked up steam and, in time, accomplished their goals and created something for the rest of the world to enjoy.

Rookery Bay National Estuarine Research Reserve in Florida is a great example. This land was once up for development with plans to build a road through the bay into the Ten Thousand Islands. This area is a natural wonder with mangrove tunnels and acres of grassy wetland that is home to alligators, rare bird species, dolphins, and manatees. A small group of concerned citizens gathered in 1964 to plot a course of action to protect the land. Their solution was to purchase it in order to protect this area, and its wild inhabitants, forever. Today, the 110,000 acres[1] of protected land has seen hundreds of thousands of sea turtles hatch and head to sea and the conservancy hospital treats and releases thousands of injured animals back to the wild.

Another fantastic example is the IncrEDIBLE initiative in Trail, British Columbia. Trail's downtown includes corridors of urban food gardens that line the sidewalks. These gardens are maintained by the local business owners and grow food such as berries, tomatoes, and cabbages for the public.

It all started when a local business owner from Trail watched a TEDTalk called "How We Can Eat Our Landscapes," by Pam Warhurst.[2] The Trail business owner was inspired after watching the video and decided to do something similar in her community. Contacting other local business owners, she rallied some interest and bought the first planters. Now, many businesses are involved and the streets are lined with greenery and food.

These are just a couple of examples of the hundreds I could put in this book, about passionate people banding together to make a difference. For generations, we have witnessed land protected due to the vigilance and persistence of small groups of informed citizens. On Vancouver Island, I have heard of very few parks that were started in

1 Rookery Bay National Estuarine Research Reserve, accessed February 2015.
  https://rookerybay.org/about-us.html
2 "How We Can Eat Our Landscapes," by Pam Warhurst, accessed February 2015.
  http://www.ted.com/talks/pam_warhurst_how_we_can_eat_our_landscapes

any other way. Now more than ever, environmental issues are a top concern and we need leaders in every area, from greening businesses to policy change and taking action in our own backyards.

Though the right course of action depends very much on the desired outcome, most successful projects evolved through a common process discussed in the following sections.

## 2.1 Get the right people in the room

It may be a jolt of inspiration; an "aha moment" that comes to you in a rush, or an old flame of an idea that you have been mulling over for years, but that spark of inspiration, new or old, is what ignites a new initiative.

Share the spark and source for inspiration with people who can help instigate the change you wish to see. They may take to it, they may not, but if you share your original source of inspiration, those with a similar perspective may see what you see as a great opportunity. Whenever I have a good idea, I make a little list on the side of people I would like to talk to about it. These are people who could help make it happen, lend advice, or share some interest.

Hosting a conversation with a group of individuals that may share your concern can be a casual gathering, or a more formal setting. Living room or boardroom, the purpose is to discuss the vision and gather input towards a shared mission. You may wish to start with a brainstorm, or use a roundtable model in which each person at the table has a chance to voice his or her concerns and share insights (limiting the time each person can have). The host should set the stage, letting everyone know why they have gathered and what the purpose of the gathering is.

For example, we recently hosted a meeting to discuss the issue of pollution coming from hair salons. Five of us gathered, including a regional district member, salon owner, water treatment technician, nonprofit employee, and Synergy representative. We told everyone, "We are here to discuss the matter of salon greening. We know that hair chemicals are toxic and they are not treated before they enter our oceans. So, we are curious to find out if there is something we can do at the source, within salons. We don't have the answers yet, and we would like to brainstorm with you to discover possibilities. You all have some sort of expertise that could lend to solving this issue." This project is now heading towards prototyping a new technology that can detoxify the rinse water at the source.

## 2.2 Clearly define the common goal

Once you have discussed the matter and heard from the stakeholders in the group, you will need to bring the ideas to a focal point, or common goal. For the salon group, the goal is to pilot a technology that will treat water right at the sink pipe, before it enters the sewage lines.

You may not have an objective that is simple, and it may be that not everyone agrees, but you will need to focus on an objective or a goal that most can visualize. This could be a new farmers' market, reducing beach plastic, adding composting systems to local residences, or lobbying for more bike lanes in the city. Whatever your common goal, write it down and share it.

## 2.3 Determine the barriers

Almost as soon as the idea becomes clear, we tend to start thinking about the obstacles. This is human nature, and they can get in our way too soon. Give barriers attention after the common goal is defined. Otherwise, the process can feel daunting and impossible, deflating your ambition and passion to make things happen. However, it is important to look ahead to determine the barriers you may come across to see your vision through. These barriers may include the following:

- **Economic:** Pricing, funding required, or negative impact on businesses.

- **Social:** Lack of will, education, perspective, time, knowledge, or belief.

- **Political:** Preventative bylaws, bureaucracy, policies, or political will.

- **Environmental:** Lack of space or poor air quality.

When you understand the barriers, it is easier to chart a path to overcome them. It can be helpful to list each potential barrier, or hurdle to achieving your goal. For example, the salon group needed to list the barriers and create an action plan, as you can see in Table 2.

Your next step is to make a plan to reconvene on a regular basis, or a predetermined time to keep the momentum rolling.

**Table 2**
## Determine the Barriers and Take Action

| Barrier | Action Plan |
|---|---|
| *Example:*<br>**Money:** Need to find funding to pilot the technology at a local salon. | *Example:*<br>Jill, Kayli, and Stephanie to make a list of potential funding sources including grants and private funding. |
| **Knowledge:** Need to conduct a study of the results in a scientific way. | Contact University professors in the area to see if they would be interested in studying the project.<br>Also contact engineering department at the city and regional district. |
| **Your Barriers** | **Your Action Plan** |
|  |  |

# 3. Outreach Tools

A project can use a variety of tools to achieve its environmental objective. What is most important is that you engage the right people. Many fantastic causes fly under the radar because the organizers do not put out the word. Communication and outreach are keys to helping you get your project started, and continuing it to successful completion.

If your project requires the buy-in from only a few individuals, fantastic, but it's more likely that your project will need to gain some exposure to be successful. Make your cause accessible for others to join with regular meetings and providing information online. Here are some communication tools at your disposal:

- Start a free online campaign using platforms such as Change. org.

- Write opinion columns in local newspapers.

- Use free e-newsletter tools such as MailChimp.com to keep people informed.

- Utilize social media to create a buzz and spread the word.

- Present to classrooms, at events, and host workshops.

These processes and tools can help you be effective in taking action to solve environmental issues. The following chapters are filled with ideas of how to make a green community, and what you can do to become part of the solution, and lead your area to a more sustainable future.

# 3
# Food Security

*Food security exists "when all people at all times have access to sufficient, safe, nutritious food to maintain a healthy and active life."*

— World Food Summit, 1996

 Food security is a complex issue linked to economic development, social welfare, human health, natural environments, and global trade. How we choose to eat can have a vast impact on the health of our planet, society, and ourselves.

The heart of our communities and cultures, food is a part of our everyday life, and it connects us. We celebrate, socialize, and plan our communities around food. Thus, to embark on a path towards greening a community, food is a great place to start.

In urban environments, people lose connection to the origin of food and the knowledge of how it is grown and how it can be prepared. With the convenience of the modern grocery store, this knowledge, once so critical to our survival, is disappearing. For reasons such as health, affordability, and emissions reductions, it is important to maintain a strong connection to the food we eat, whether we live in the countryside or in a metropolis.

In the processing and transportation of food products, nutritional value is lost and preservatives must be added. These long-traveled foods often come in hefty packaging and carry with them a high carbon footprint. In addition, we lose connection to who grew our food and how. These concerns have captured the attention of citizens and are the root of the Global Fair Trade and Organic Certification movements. All this to say, growing food close to home is good for many reasons: You gain access to high-quality fresh foods with a lower environmental footprint while building meaningful connections to foods origins.

## 1. Growing Food Locally

There are several factors that contribute to food's environmental impact, including: How low on the food chain it is, how it is grown, and how far it travels. The David Suzuki Foundation states that "the average meal travels 1,200 kilometers [746 miles] from the farm to plate."[1]

Building a local food community has a variety of benefits:

- Builds community, connecting farmers and neighbors.
- Creates jobs and contributes to a local economy with value-added products.
- Preserves farmlands and ecosystems.
- Lower carbon footprint
- Food is fresher and tastes better.
- Local, diverse crops preserve genetic diversity.

The following are some actions you can take to help build your local food community:

- Start a Food Box program at school or work to make local food accessible. Food Box programs typically deliver fresh produce directly from a farm on a regular basis through the growing season. Boxes are sold at a fixed price and are delivered directly to the consumer, or hub such as a school or workplace.
- Grow your own garden. Even a small patio garden can supply you with the herbs you need for your cooking. Larger gardens can yield enough vegetables and starches to reduce your grocery bill in half or more during harvest season.

---

1 "Food and Climate Change," David Suzuki Foundation, accessed February 2015.
   http://www.davidsuzuki.org/what-you-can-do/food-and-our-planet/food-and-climate-change/

- Shop at your local farmers' market or start one!

- Distribute a calendar of seasonal foods with a list of local food providers to friends and family.

- Support restaurants that use local ingredients.

- Start a community garden in your neighborhood or at a local school, church, or other gathering place.

## 2. The Environmental Impact of Meat

A pound of beef requires about seven pounds of feed, compared to more than three pounds for a pound of pork and less than two pounds for a pound of chicken.[2] This does not take into account the waste in processing the meat to what we buy on the shelves. These feed-to-meat ratios can change significantly; however, based on the type of feed and how the animal was "finished," which is the diet for the 90 to 120 days before slaughter. Although there are many factors at play, one thing is for sure: The environmental impact of eating meat is the exponentially higher than the impact of eating grains and vegetables.

Raising animals for human consumption accounts for a staggering 40 percent of the total amount of agricultural output in developed countries. Feed crops alone use about one-third of all arable land on the planet. It can be hard to imagine the thousands of acres of livestock that exists to fuel our urban areas, but they exist. These acres are simply displaced — elsewhere in the world, spread over plains and areas that were once rain forests. In Latin America, 70 percent of what was once forested land has now been converted to pastures and feed crops.

**Important Note:** Livestock production accounts for 70 percent of all agricultural land and 30 percent of the land surface of the planet.[3]

Climate change is another major concern relating to livestock production. Methane is a powerful greenhouse gas (23 times stronger than carbon dioxide), and is produced in the digestive systems of cattle and other livestock. Yes, they produce gas, like most creatures, and it happens to have a high Global Warming Potential (GWP). Livestock also produced ammonia (which causes acid rain) and nitrous oxide (another powerful greenhouse gas) from manure.

---

2  "How the Chicken Conquered the World," Jerry Adler and Andrew Lawler (June 2012), Smithsonian, accessed March 2015. http://www.smithsonianmag.com/history/how-the-chicken-conquered-the-world-87583657/?no-ist

3  *Livestock's Long Shadow: Environmental Issues and Options*, H. Steinfeld, P. Gerber, T. Wassenaar, V. Castel, M. Rosales, C. Haan (2006); Livestock, Environment and Development, FAO, Rome. Retrieved March 2015

This is not intended to preach a certain diet or lifestyle. Personally, I am not a vegetarian. However, understanding these impacts has changed how I shop and plan meals. When my partner and I discovered the vast impact of meat, we decided to cut back. We got on board with "Meatless Monday" and started to find alternatives to adding meat to our dishes. We bought vegetarian cookbooks to make vegetarian meals taste just as good, or better, than if they had been made with meat.

If a community reduces the meat they consume by a few percent as a portion of its total diet, it can significantly reduce carbon emissions and stresses on ecosystems.

The following are some actions you can take to reduce meat consumption:

- Institute "Meatless Mondays," or commit to eating two meatless meals per day.

- Raise awareness on World Vegetarian Day (October 1).

- Support restaurants with vegetarian, locally grown options.

## 3. The Environmental Impact of Seafood

*"A combination of public commitment and bold input by scientists can be powerful in reducing threats to marine life, particularly when a government is failing to protect."*

— Amanda C. J. Vincent and Jean M. Harris,
Marine Science Experts

Issues that put our marine ecosystems at risk include overfishing, habitat loss, climate change, and fishing methods. For decades, populations of fish have been dwindling, though they have a remarkable ability to bounce back when given the chance. Before 2050 it is estimated that there will be 9 billion people on the planet.[4] Seafood is a rich source or protein and nutrients that many nations rely on. In countries such as Iceland, Portugal, Japan, and China, fish is a huge part of the daily diet.

About 75 percent of the world-fish catch is used for human consumption. The remainder is converted into fish meal and oil used mainly for animal feed (including farmed fish).[5] For this reason, it

---

4 "International Data Base World Population: 1950–2050," United States Census Bureau, accessed March 2015. http://www.census.gov/population/international/data/idb/worldpopgraph.php
5 "Who Eats Fish?" Food and Agriculture Organization of the United Nations, accessed March 2015. http://www.fao.org/focus/e/fisheries/consum.htm

is important to consider eating lower on the food chain. When you consider the mass amount of other species it takes to produce say, one tuna fish, the impact of human seafood consumption rises exponentially. Compare to eating lower on the food chain, seafood such as sardines, crabs, mussels, shrimp, and others are fast reproducers and require less environmental input to produce a meals' worth of protein.

For consumers to support and promote healthy oceans, eco-certifications such as Ocean Wise can help identify which species and sources are more sustainably harvested. Most of these certifications focus on industrial-scale fishing practices, which is a major global concern.

New research has shone the light on a large segment of the fishing industry that often flies under the radar, which is at the community level. The small, local fisheries are present in almost every coastal community. These ubiquitous fisheries may seem like they dwarf in comparison to large industrial fisheries, but cumulatively they have an enormous impact on life in the waters.

A study by Vincent and Harris, recently published in *Science*, found that small-scale fisheries involve about 90 percent of the world's fishers.[6] Bringing small fisheries to the attention of science and academia, this study points to what we can do at a community level to protect and restore fisheries. By working with small-scale fishers on best practices, new methods, protection zones, sustainable management, and regulatory practices, we can act now for healthy oceans and freshwater systems in the future.

One major issue the study points to is the use of bottom-trolling, which results on destruction of the ocean floor and bycatch (accidental catchment of nontargeted species). The article says, "Of all indiscriminate fisheries, bottom trawling is the most catastrophic for both species and habitats. It also contributes substantially to Illegal Unregulated and Unreported Fishing (IUU) take, mainly through bycatch. Even where a trawl fishery for the target species is legal — and they often are not — the other marine life it captures is very rarely regulated or reported. Yet thousands of animal, plant, and algal species are taken incidentally. Cumulatively, they often constitute 85 to 90% of the total biomass of the catch in the net."

It is clear that we need to focus on both the large, industrial-scale fisheries and the small-scale fisheries where much activity is unregulated or unnoticed.

6 "Boundless No More," Amanda C. J. Vincent, and Jean M. Harris (Science 24. Oct 2014. Vol. 346 no. 6208 pp. 420-421 DOI: 10.1126/science.1255923), accessed March 2015.

We can take action in our own communities to protect water life, first by raising awareness in the community on topics such as species loss, sustainable fishing methods, water pollution, the impact of climate change, and the economic value of a sustainable fishery. We can rally for change by working in collaborative groups that involve government, industry, conservation groups, and more. Schools are a fantastic platform to raise awareness — get children and teachers engaged in lessons about sustainable fisheries, and outdoor activities that facilitate preservation such as beach cleanups, removal of invasive species, sign-making, fundraising, and exploring natural areas.

Anyone can start a group or project that begins to make a difference. You can also shop for sustainable seafood and share resources to help other consumers support eco-certifications.

Governance at a community level plays a critical role in fisheries management in your community and worldwide. "What we know from the failure of management schemes globally is that regulation at the national level is not enough. Every layer of government, including regions and communities, must help small-scale fishers get control of the fisheries on which they depend," says Harris in the report.

In addition, protecting marine environments, and gaining support for no-take zones can help reestablish populations, allowing them to regain numbers. These zones can be nurseries for fish and other species, and can drastically change the fate of a fishery.

The solution to a sustainable global fishery is leadership at both the local and global level. In communities that have set a shining example for the rest of the world, action was taken by a few engaged and active citizens to see change and shift the tides towards overfishing to sustainable fishing. Your community can do the same.

Here are some solutions:

- Promote the Ocean Wise Sustainable Seafood program in your local community, and encourage restaurants and seafood retailers to get on board (www.oceanwise.ca).

- Look for seafood that is rated best choice by SeaChoice, which means they are caught or grown in a more environmentally sustainable manner (www.seachoice.org).

- Eat lower on the food chain (e.g., shellfish rather than tuna or swordfish).

- Help remove pollution from beaches.

- Encourage collaboration between academic, government, non-profit, and business communities in your area to promote sustainable fishing practices.

- Support and promote policies that encourage sustainable seafood harvesting practices locally and internationally.

- Educate consumers about what species are threatened and endangered — distribute lists.

- Read about the Slow Food Campaign: Understanding the Oceans (www.slowfood.com/slowfish).

---

**Conservation Project**
False Creek Herring Restoration

North of Vancouver, British Columbia, a small group of volunteers have restored a long-lost herring population in False Creek, which flows into the Pacific Ocean. They wrapped the pilings of docks with a mesh-like material so the herring eggs could stick to the surface, rather than having the spawn wash away. For the first time in decades, millions of herring spawned into the creek.[7] The herring spawn is important for coastal birds, bears, salmon, and dozens of other species that feed on the eggs and hatched herring. Revitalizing the herring is like giving the whole coastal ecosystem a boost. This technique is now being considered in dozens of coastal harbors to bring back the herring.

---

# 4. Food Waste

According to a policy brief issued in 2008 by the Food and Agriculture Organization of the United Nations, close to half of all food produced is wasted in transit, at grocery stores, and in our kitchens. The authors state that the food crisis we may face is not one of production, but one of waste. The policy brief asks governments to reduce food waste in half by 2025.[8] Food waste is increased as the steps to process and ship the food increase. It is also something to be aware of in your own home, work functions, and schools.

---

7  "Pollution Thwarts Efforts to Restore False Creek Herring Population," Matthew Robinson, *The Vancouver Sun* (September 26, 2014), accessed March 2015. http://www.vancouver-sun.com/news/Pollution+thwarts+efforts+restore+False+Creek+herring+populat ion/10240095/story.html#ixzz3TrNdkCkW
8  "Saving Water: From Field to Fork — Curbing Losses and Wastage in the Food Chain," J. Lundqvist, C. de Fraiture, and D. Molden, SIWI Policy Brief, SIWI 2008, accessed March 2015. http://www.siwi.org/documents/Resources/Policy_Briefs/PB_From_Filed_to_Fork_2008.pdf

Another trending topic is the amount of food that is discarded due to a slight imperfection in shape, skin texture, color, or minor bruises. Failure to meet rigid quality inspections means this perfectly edible and equally nutritious food is used for feed, dumped, or tilled back into the soil. As a result, we reject an apple for not having the perfect "apple" shape. These strict aesthetic screens prevent us from eating much of the food that yields from crops, wasting precious soil, water, and energy inputs. A grocer in Australia called Harris Farm Markets has reacted to this issue, launching the Imperfect Picks Campaign, which is designed to reduce food waste by selling "ugly" fruit and vegetables that might otherwise have been rejected.[9]

Similarly, a French supermarket called Intermarché aims to change our perspective on misshapen fruit and vegetables with a campaign launched in 2014 with a mission to end food waste. The third largest supermarket chain in France, Intermarché, is no small player, and their Inglorious Fruits and Vegetables campaign has turned the tables, celebrating imperfections in food that still has quality nutrition. The campaign features posters of unattractive produce with witty slogans: Ugly Carrot: In a Soup, Who Cares, and A Hideous Orange: Makes Beautiful Juice.

The imperfect fruit and vegetables were sold at 30 percent less than their perfect counterparts and the result was a big success. The imperfect options were a popular choice and the supermarket traffic increased overall by 24 percent.[10]

Offering healthy, yet imperfect, fruits and vegetables can also help make quality, nutritious food more affordable to those that need it. To combat food waste, enhance food security, and affordability, we need to make room for the imperfect yields in our grocery stores and shopping baskets.

Here are some actions you can take to help prevent food waste:

- Use smart shopping rules in your household such as buying only what you need.

- Manage your fridge to keep things clean, organized, and easy to manage.

9 "Harris Farm Markets Grocer launches 'Imperfect Picks' Campaign," Sophie Langley (September 15, 2014), *Australian Food News (AFN)*, access March 2015. http://ausfoodnews.com.au/2014/09/15/harris-farm-markets-grocer-launches-imperfect-picks-campaign.html
10 "Forget the Ugli Fruit, Meet the Ugly Fruit Bowl! French Supermarket Introduces Lumpy and Misshapen Fruit and Vegetables — Sold at a 30% Discount — to Combat Food Waste," Martha Cliff (July 16, 2014), *MailOnline*, accessed March 2015. http://www.dailymail.co.uk/femail/food/article-2693000/Forget-ugli-fruit-meet-ugly-fruit-bowl-French-supermarket-introduces-lumpy-misshapen-fruit-vegetables-sold-30-discount-combat-food-waste.html#ixzz3TrYygkeD

- Educate your kids, housemates, and friends about food waste and challenge them to reduce.

- Encourage grocery stores to stock and reduce the price of imperfect fruits and vegetables.

- Organize a "clean plate" campaign to raise awareness about food waste and encourage people to take only what they need. This is especially effective in places with cafeterias and all-you-can-eat buffets.

- Speak with your local government about food-waste-reduction policies.

- Suggest to local restaurants to offer half or smaller portion options.

## 5. Community Gardening

Community gardens are very popular in dense neighborhoods where people in condominiums or apartments may not have ground space for growing. They are also popular at universities, urban residential areas, and in seniors' areas. Community gardens have many benefits. They create a sense of place, with opportunities to socialize and meet neighbors. They provide educational opportunities for children and adults who also gain physical fitness by working in a garden that grows local, fresh, and affordable food. Not to mention, gardens are aesthetically pleasing and can beautify an area.

Community gardens have become a global movement, with gardens in countries around the world. Montreal, Canada, has more than 100 garden sites with thousands of participants.

How do they start? They identify a potential area. It may be city property, such as a nearby park, school property, or development lands. Others have been started in old parking lots. Note that the organization or individual who owns the land will need to agree that the land can be used by a community group, or the public, for growing food.

Often the land is divided into plots, which are then allocated to individuals. Community gardens typically have a loose structure of rules and regulations that must be abided by in order to keep the gardens active and maintained properly. Thus, community gardens are spaces of collaboration and working together. In a sense, they are their own mini-communities, and they foster sharing of assets (e.g., tools, equipment), knowledge, and new friendships. They give their members a sense of pride and accomplishment, along with the ability to provide for themselves, even in a small way.

In urban environments, where access to land is expensive or nearly impossible to find, community gardens provide a place to learn how to grow and harvest food; these important life skills are kept alive in the community garden space. The beauty aspect of community garden spaces may seem like a small side-benefit, but it can be quite profound. It can increase the value of nearby property and improve the views of those living in buildings in the area. It can block traffic views and offer a quiet, peaceful aesthetic to an urban jungle. Effectively, community gardens are not just for the gardeners, they are for the passersby, the residences in the area, and the visitors, too.

Gardening is a healthy, meditative exercise that can reduce stress, which is why gardens are becoming more common in special care homes, hospitals, and senior centers. Garden beds can be raised to waist height to make them easier to access from a wheelchair and/ or reduce back strain from bending down to weed and harvest the plants. In sum, community gardens are a healthy way to make use of barren land, bring people together; and promote healthy lifestyles, beautiful cities, social cohesion, and food security.

## 5.1 Guerilla gardening

Guerilla gardening has become a popular activism statement in which gardeners use land that they legally do not have the right to use. This can go well, or it can go badly. Either the organization who owns the property sees the beauty and bounty and allows the garden to exist; or the hard work is bulldozed. Guerilla gardening can be seen as a statement, and in its extreme, a form of vandalism, or it can be seen as positive community action.

In Australia, a group called "Permablitz" gather regularly to construct urban vegetable gardens for free, in an effort to educate residents on how to grow their own food. Some guerilla garden acts have taken place at night, transforming an area to draw media attention and raise awareness about food security. While guerilla gardening has been successful at taking a stand and getting many urban garden projects off the ground, there is a growing uptake from government and other landowners to make use of wasted land space — community gardens are becoming popular in cities all over the world. Working with permission is always better, but sometimes, a risky act to demonstrate what is possible is a powerful message to those who may not see the beauty or need for food growing in urban and suburban areas.

## 5.2 Sharing backyards

Backyard gardening is nothing new, but it was less common near the end of the 20th century as yards became more ornamental statements, rather than edible landscapes that provide sustenance. However, the tides are changing again and garden beds are popping up in backyards to grow fresh greens, fruits, and vegetables.

While backyard gardening is picking up again, some people simply do not have the time or know-how to make the effort themselves, so many yards are underutilized by a busy working family. Some may think, wouldn't it be great if someone would come here and turn this into a producing garden and share the produce? Well, that's what sharing backyard programs are all about. Essentially, it is a matchmaking between people who have yards, and people who want to garden but do not have access to a yard. Yard owners can offer garden space in exchange for part of the bounty and gardeners can access a plot free of cost.

Similarly, many people have properties with fruit trees that are not fully harvested and utilized when the fruit is ripe. I lived in a place that had three apple trees and I can tell you that even with picking one-third of the fruit, I could not make enough apple crumble, pies, and jelly without quitting my job to focus on processing those apples. This is the case for many of the producing fruit trees on private property. Much of the fruit simply drops, rots, and goes to waste. Instead, that fresh, local fruit could have gone to those in need.

The LifeCycles Fruit Tree Project in Victoria allows people to register their fruit tree online, and a group of volunteers comes by to pick the fruit at harvest time and share it among home owners, volunteers, food banks, and community organizations. In 2014, LifeCycles collected and distributed 30,000 pounds of fruit![11]

The following are some actions you can take to build a community garden:

- Build educational gardens at local schools.

- Start a community garden in your area.

- Start a backyard gardening and "sharing backyard" programs

- Request a local bylaw allowing for curbside gardens (between sidewalk and road).

11 LifeCycles Fruit Tree Project, accessed March 2015. http://lifecyclesproject.ca/initiatives/fruit_tree/

- Plant fruit or nut trees instead of ornamental plants.

For further information, check out the following:

- American Community Gardening Association: https://community garden.org/

- City Farmer News: http://www.cityfarmer.info/

## 6. Urban Agriculture

According to American Farmland Trust, "In America, we've been losing more than an acre of farmland per minute."[12]

Many of our grocery store foods contain ingredients grown in tropical regions (e.g., palm, coconut, soy). In many cases, rain forest areas, some of the biologically richest areas in the world, are cut down to grow these crops. This is part of the reason why growing at least some of our food within our local communities is so important.

An inspiring example of urban agriculture is in Prairie Crossing, Chicago.[13] This subdivision hosts a 100-acre farm at the heart of the development. Instead of tennis or golf, this area brings people together who enjoy the lifestyle of casual farming. The developers wanted to create a return on their investment, but they also wanted to conserve the land. Liberty Prairie Foundation[14] is a nonprofit that runs the garden and is partly funded by the proceeds from the sales of the homes. Prior to development there were ten bird species found on the land. Now there are more than 100 due to the establishment of a wetland zone for storm-water management. Young farmers can rent five-acre parcels of land and this lease helps aspiring farmers overcome cost barriers.

More developers have since picked up on this idea. Liberty Prairie Foundation is setting an example worldwide for how to create a profitable subdivision community centered around food security and a back-to-the-land lifestyle that many families desire.

## 7. Urban Livestock

Gardening and providing for your family is rewarding and helps reduce the environmental impacts that result through the conventional food supply chain. In addition to fruits and vegetables, more people are bringing the farm to the city by introducing urban livestock and poultry.

12 "Threatened Farmland: What's Happening to Our Farmland?" American Farmland Trust, accessed March 2015. http://www.farmland.org/resources/fote/
13 Prairie Crossing, accessed February 2015. http://www.prairiecrossing.com/
14 Liberty Prairie Foundation, accessed February 2015. http://libertyprairie.org/

Goats, chickens, and ducks are common in today's urban micro-farm.

When it comes to raising animals on your urban property, municipal bylaws come into play. Some have old or new bylaws that allow for backyard chickens, for example, while others do not allow any poultry or livestock on urban properties. Municipalities must assess the risks to introducing a policy or bylaw by examining public health issues, the needs of the community, and codes of practice for keeping animals healthy. The City of Vancouver recently introduced a bylaw to allow for backyard chickens (no ducks, turkeys, goats, or other livestock). The bylaw allows for up to four hens (no roosters) and the hens must be registered on the City of Vancouver's online system. The eggs and hens cannot be sold commercially, and the size and location of the coop must follow specific guidelines to be sure the hens are treated humanely and to respect the neighborhood.

Chickens are social creatures, so it is important to have more than one, or she is likely to die from the stress of being alone. They can live up to ten years, so they are a considerable commitment; however, the fresh eggs and the self-sufficiency can be worth it.

On a neighborhood level, policies and bylaws that allow for backyard chickens promote food security by allowing citizens to maintain access to a consistent, fresh supply of organic eggs. In addition, chickens consume kitchen scraps, which reduces the amount of waste that needs to be hauled by municipal services. Chicken manure is also a nutrient-rich fertilizer for use in flower and vegetable gardens.

Some concerns for municipalities that introduce backyard chicken programs include:

- Attracting wildlife to the city such as coyotes, raccoons, and cougars.

- Noise and smell of chickens.

- Food safety regarding the smell of unregulated eggs.

- Bylaw enforcement costs.

---

### Easy Project: A Potato Bumper Crop on your Patio!

Growing potatoes in a space as small as a single-square foot is possible and easy. This is a great project if you have a small balcony or deck. As a bonus, you will be recycling used materials to make your potato garden.

To begin your garden you will need a bag of rich soil, a used shopping bag, three or four sprouting potatoes (this happens when you buy a potato and accidentally leave in on your counter for a week or two — it will begin to sprout from the nodes). For the bag, you can use a thicker plastic shopping bag or a regular black garbage bag.

Structure the bag so it is flat on the bottom and cut a few X shapes with scissors into the bottom of the bag so it can drain excess water. Next, put a few inches of soil into the bag. Then place your potato sprouts on the soil, evenly spaced apart. Next, cover the potatoes with another few inches of soil. Water lightly, and place outside to grow.

When the plants have grown to 12 to 16 inches, add more soil, covering the base. Continue to do this as the plant grows until the bag is almost full. Water regularly and in the fall, simply dump your bag of soil upside down into another bag or sheet of plastic and harvest your fresh potatoes.

---

## 8. Farming Food Instead of Manicuring Lawns

Lawns are a curious fascination of our modern day culture. Inspired by the grand estates of 19th century England, when lawns were a sign of wealth and importance, we began to place our homes on mini-estate-like surroundings. This has become the norm and is no longer reserved for the most grandeur castles. On the NASA Earth Observatory website, a research group directed by Dr. Cristina Milesi, estimates that "there are three times more acres of lawns in the US than irrigated corn" and that lawn area covers "about 128,000 square kilometers in all."[15] The area of land dedicated to lawn is now more than that dedicated to food crops such as corn and wheat!

As North American nations, we obsess over lawns — millions and millions of acres of them. We spend time, money, and effort to maintain their perfection. While they create green space, lawns are a biological wasteland due to the presence of a single species of plant, and the fertilization and pesticides they need. Not only are lawns costly to us, they are costly on the environment. Moving and trimming equipment burns fossil fuels and causes air pollution and noise. The Environmental Protection Agency (EPA) estimates that up to one-third of residential water is used for lawn care.[16] The pesticides and fertilizers

15 "Looking for Lawns," Rebecca Lindsey, NASA Earth Observatory, accessed February 2015. http://earthobservatory.nasa.gov/Features/Lawn/lawn.php
16 "Outdoor Water Use in the United States," WaterSense and the United States

used to maintain lawns washes into waterways, causing chemical imbalances that create dead zones in local lakes, rivers, and oceans.

Growing awareness of the environmental impact of lawns has resulted in an anti-lawn movement that favors natural landscapes and native plant gardens that support many species and require no watering, maintenance hours, or chemicals to survive. In some neighborhoods, it is mandatory to have a lawn and keep it green. However, if you do have the option to change your landscaping, consider planting native varieties and/or food gardens.

Here are some actions you can take to grow more food and less lawn:

- Stage the replacement of grass with native plant gardens and/or food gardens.

- Start a campaign to create awareness about the impact of lawns.

- Communicate your views on lawns to your local politicians and request that policies reflect the shift from lawns to native plants and food gardens.

## 9. Stop Using Pesticides

Bees are arguably one the most important insects on the planet when it comes to food production. Without bees, we would not only lose honey, we would lose fruit trees, nuts, and vegetables. Pollination is absolutely vital to the food web, and bees are the world's number one pollinator.

The decline in bee populations in recent decades has deeply frightened both farmers and biologists. Without the bees, how we will grow oranges, almonds, and apples? And what on Earth will we do without honey? The potential loss of bees is a real threat to our food production and our natural world.

Why are bees dying? This phenomenon puzzled biologists for years, and we still don't have all the answers, but there is one thing we do know. Pesticides that we use on our lawns kill bees. You can take action to help reduce excessive pesticide use and help save pollinators such as bees and butterflies:

- Start a campaign for "Pesticide Free Lawns."

- Ask your landscaper to avoid using pesticides.

Environmental Protection Agency (EPA), accessed March 2015.
http://www.epa.gov/WaterSense/pubs/outdoor.html

- Plant pollinator-friendly plants such as native wildflowers with yellow, white, blue, and purple flowers; or food plants such as squash, foxglove, lavender, blueberry, and blackberry.

- Install a bee bath in your yard, with rocks and a shallow pool of water.

- Educate your local community about the value of pollinators.

- Introduce pollinator and pesticide education in local schools.

- Turn your curbside or corridor into a food garden.

- Support local beekeepers and purchase locally made honey.

**Fun Facts:** Hummingbirds are also important pollinators and they are attracted to tubular red flowers. Bees are attracted to flowers with a solid foundation they can land on (e.g., sunflowers).

# 4
# Green Events

One of the most anticipated events in our hometown of Victoria is the Rifflandia Music Festival. Artists, vendors, and party-thirsty patrons fill a downtown park for three days. The event brings the whole town together and amplifies the culture of our city.

Similar to Victoria, many communities have a special annual event — one that celebrates everything that makes that town unique. For Nanaimo, it's the annual Bathtub Race, where bathtubs of all kinds are motored across the ocean to the beaches of Vancouver. Avon, Ohio, hosts the Avon Heritage Duct Tape Festival, with a parade of floats made of duct tape. Every spring, Pikeville, Kentucky, celebrates Hillbilly Days with all manners of hillbilly lifestyle. Every community hosts events to celebrate and entertain with music, sports, arts, or things like lentils (Pullman, Washington). Whatever the event, they bring us together and create a sense of place by animating our lifestyles, our culture, and the things we appreciate.

While these events bring our communities to life, dense congregations of people are prone to creating a lot of waste and using vast amounts of energy. The Environmental Protection Agency (EPA) has noted marketing, hotel stays, food services, and exhibitions as major sources of waste generated from events such as meetings and conferences. Events can also be huge energy consumers. Add the greenhouse gas emissions from all the travel to get to an event and the environmental impact begins to look scary. That's not to say we shouldn't have events, but we should look at how to reduce the environmental impact of our community events.

Large events, such as conferences, sport competitions, and music festivals can be a major source of greenhouse gas emissions. Even birthday parties and weddings can use a lot of natural resources. With some simple changes to planning and purchasing, the environmental impact of an event can be drastically reduced, which is why we have a chapter in this book dedicated to green events.

In many communities, greening events are low-hanging-fruit projects with big results. So how do you begin? Fortunately, there are some great examples of green events around the world that have achieved zero waste and used 100 percent renewable energy sources (see section 3.).

Because events bring people together, they are ideal opportunities for demonstrating environmental leadership. Stewardship can start with events. You can work to make your community events green, or host new events specifically for environmental causes. We will discuss both of these opportunities in this chapter.

## 1. Community Events

A green event is an opportunity for every community, whether there are 500 people or 500 million in your area. Green event practices can be applied to the following:

- Festivals.

- Parades.

- Conferences.

- Sports events and races.

- Markets.

- Concerts and shows.

- Fairs and carnivals.

Eco-friendly parties and events are becoming a major trend, and they can look fabulous. Many guests like knowing that they aren't creating huge amounts of waste at an event they are attending, and appreciate the thoughtfulness of planning a green party.

The key to planning an environmentally friendly event is to integrate environmental priorities early on in the event planning. Right from the outset, aim to make your event exemplary of how events can tread lightly on the planet. Incorporate these environmental principals in every area of planning, from food to flyers:

- Reduce waste wherever possible through product choosing, reuse, repurposing, and recycling.

- Support your local, greener economy in the products and services you use for your event.

- Reduce your carbon footprint by planning green transportation options and consuming less energy.

- Educate attendees about green options and engage them in the process

Checklist 1 shows you the many aspects to consider for a greener event.

## 2. Family Events

You can even consider going green for family events such as birthday parties, reunions, and weddings. Think about the most recent child's birthday party you attended. Chances are you saw a lot of disposable dishware and decor, enough to fill a garbage bag or two or three. Eco-friendly party planning is becoming easier with more reusable and compostable products available. You can decorate with natural and reusable materials as well.

Then there all the toys and favors; for example, I remember goodie bags as a kid, and many were toys for a moment, then they were trash. Parties are loaded with disposable items, but there are simple ways to reduce trash and wasted money; for example, when buying banners and signs, buy durable ones that say "Happy Birthday," "Happy Halloween," or "Happy New Year" without a year or date so they can be reused.

Gifts are another big waste generator. The week after Christmas, streets are lined with bags upon bags of ribbon, wrapping, bows, and tape for curbside garbage pick up. The good news is, people are becoming somewhat conscious about the waste they are making and we are starting to see some reductions, but there is far more we can do

## Checklist 1
### Planning Considerations for a Green Event

**Location**

○ Choose a green building for your venue, and seek naturally lit rooms or host your event outdoors.

○ Destination is central to attendees and accessible by sustainable transportation.

○ Prioritize a location with easy access to transit, bike paths, or other means of sustainable transport.

**Energy and Water**

○ Supplement energy requirements with a clean power source such as biodiesel generators or solar panels. If these are not available, consider purchasing green energy credits from organizations such as BullFrog Power.

○ Have water fountains and water-refill stations to avoid plastic water bottles.

**Decorating**

○ Ditch the balloons because they are temporary, disposable decor that rarely gets recycled and often ends up in streams, oceans, and other natural environments where they cause harm to wildlife (see BalloonsBlow.org).

○ Use living centerpieces such as potted flowers, succulents or herbs, and recycled vases or containers such as wine bottles or wooden boxes.

○ Go with a more natural theme. Consider all of your decorating items; for example, if they were tossed in the forest, could they decompose and become food again? Use natural resources such as wood, linen, beeswax, and flowers.

**Paper**

○ Print flyers, posters, and programs on post-consumer recycled paper, and Forest Stewardship Council (FSC) certified.

○ Reduce size of flyers, posters, programs, and other materials to reduce printing.

○ Print double-sided whenever possible.

○ Distribute one program for every one or three attendees, instead of to every individual.

### Transportation

○ Provide bicycle parking for people to arrive via sustainable transportation.

○ Organize shuttle service to major junctures to reduce the need for parking and vehicle travel to the event.

### Waste Management

○ Have recycling and composting receptacles along with trash (make trash a "last resort" bin).

○ Recycle soft plastics, glass, metals, and other items.

○ Offer finger food to negate the need for disposable cutlery.

○ Have reusable or compostable plates, napkins, flatware, and cups.

○ Consider selling or providing reusable drink containers.

### Food and Beverage

○ Host with local, seasonal, and organic foods and beverages.

○ Implement "vendor sustainability criteria" for carrying compostable, recyclable, and reusable dishware. Vendors such as hotdog stands, lemonade carts, and others can generate huge amounts of waste and use a lot of energy. Your event can specify that the vendor use sustainable products in order to reduce the impact of your event.

○ Seafood served is Ocean Wise certified.

○ Have plated meals rather than buffets to avoid mass amounts of wasted food. If you do have a buffet, bring containers to allow people to take leftovers home with them.

○ Offer vegetarian options (meat typically has a higher carbon footprint).

○ Buy in bulk to reduce your plastic and metal consumption. Avoid individual packaged items wherever possible.

### Educating Attendees

○ Let guests know ahead of time that you are planning a green event, and outline what they can do to help.

○ On site, have signage showing the activities that are reducing environmental impact at the event.

○ Engage attendees in an activity such as collecting name badges for recycling, organizing a bicycle convoy, or completing a survey on green events.

on a personal level to reduce waste from gifts during Christmas, weddings, birthdays, or any other celebration.

Here are a few quick tips for greener gift giving:

- Save paper wrapping, bows, and ribbons for a craft, or to reuse clean pieces for next year.

- Chose edible or universally useful items, rather than disposable toys and favors.

- Use fabric, reusable gift wrap that can be reused for many years.

- Wrap with newspapers, magazines, your child's art, or comics.

- Offer a gift receipt for exchange, if needed.

- Give something handmade, from recycled materials (e.g., you could make a key rack using recycled wood as the backing).

- Offer your help as a gift (e.g., whatever skills you have: mechanical, cooking, decorating, building).

- Try to shop for gifts with minimal packaging to avoid the holiday waste.

- Donate cash or your time to a cause the gift receiver is passionate about. Check out JustGive.org or TheGiftofGiving.com for causes around the world.

## 3. Zero-Trash Events

Some events have taken a stand on waste by becoming completely zero-trash events. This is a great achievement that sets a positive example for the whole community. In my town, I saw how one music festival was able to accomplish this, proving to other event planners and hosts that it can be done. They shared their planning and results through a blog and website, and started a movement towards greener events. Now, it is expected that large events in the area will have proper recycling and composting at the very least, but someone had to show it was possible.

It may be challenging to make your event zero trash at first, but it will have many benefits. Participants appreciate the effort to reduce waste and they can learn about how different materials are recycled. Also, you will have no trash-hauling fees and you will deal with less waste after the event is over.

To get to zero trash, it is important to manage the different waste streams. You should consider two things:

1. Reducing the amount of waste that is produced.

2. Making sure all waste is recyclable or compostable. Nothing trashed.

Wherever you can, reduce the need to produce waste and then recycle the rest. For example, typical events create huge amounts of waste from paper cups. The lids, straws, and cups are all tossed in the trash. Think about football games, parades, fairs, and festivals — millions of cups are trashed every year from these events. An event can reduce waste by simply not offering the lids and straws, and using cups that are compostable. You can offer a discount to people who bring their own cups. Reward the behavior you want to see from patrons with financial incentives or special treatment; it's the most effective way.

To get attendees on board, let them know ahead of time that you are planning a zero-trash event. Let them know what they will need to bring to avoid trash. For example, if you don't plan to offer bottled water, advise guests that they should bring their own, or expect to buy a reusable bottle on site.

The Otalith Music Festival, which started in 2013 in Ucluelet, British Columbia, is a great example of a zero-trash event. The organizers decided the event would be as close to zero waste as possible. In order to reduce the need for plastic cups and water bottles, the organizers ordered custom-made stainless steel Klean Kanteen™ cups with the Otalith logo. When customers bought tickets to the event, they had the option to buy the stainless steel cup for $10. They were told ahead of time that they can either bring their own cup, or buy an Otalith one. The cups were a big success because they not only reduced the waste by more than 50 percent, they now have branded merchandise in cupboards all over the province. This memorabilia is good branding, and they chose something that is durable and can be reused hundreds of times.

Waste will also come from vendors, such as food and beverage carts. As a part of their registration to be a part of the event, communicate the type of flatware, cups, and cutlery they can use. Be as prescriptive as possible and be clear about what materials are not allowed at the event. All should be either compostable or recyclable, depending on the waste-management streams you will have available.

If sourcing different packing materials is an issue, offer information about what suppliers carry eco-friendly options where vendors can make their purchases. Help your vendors make the switch, and suggest that they limit their waste by only using wrapping that is necessary, and having bulk condiments available for customers. Vendors may have to add an incremental fee to their food or drink items to cover the premium cost for compostable dishware. If this is the case, encourage vendors to also offer a discount for people who bring their own cup or food containers.

To manage these expectations and plan for a seamless green event, organize a "Green Team" to work on vendor relations, waste management on-site, energy and water conservation, and customer education. Your green team should start as soon as possible, to integrate trash-free concepts and communications into the early planning stages.

Here are some fun ideas:

- Use poker chips or wooden tokens in place of paper drink tickets that get thrown away. The chips act as a currency for drinks or meals and can be used as a dollar value for different combinations. You can use them over again for future events.

- Add some flare to your event by making pennant strings out of used wrapping paper, burlap, butcher paper, scrap fabric, or other recycled material.

- Use old corks or pine cones for name-card holders at weddings or dinner events. You can also use leaves with gold or black ink for name placements.

- Use squash, greenery, and potted plants for centerpieces and decor.

## 4. Environmental Action Events

Learning about environmental issues and the devastation of our ecosystems can be depressing. I have seen too many colleagues become overwhelmed with the issues and retreat by saying, "Well, it's just too big, there is nothing I can do about it." To me, this is the greatest threat to our future. Not pollution, deforestation, or climate change, but the risk of our bright, able population to toss in the towel because it becomes too overwhelming. A professor once told me, "The greatest cure for despair is action" and that resonated with me to the core. If we band together and show leadership, we can accomplish anything. A small group of concerned individuals can change the mindset and awareness of an entire town. Events that celebrate environmental causes are a great starting point.

It wasn't until World Oceans Day (June 8) that I learned about the importance of educating children at a young age about the marine environment. It was a fabulous event! Fisherman's Wharf in Victoria was full of tourists and locals of all ages to view the marine wildlife, donate to the cause, and see the seals through underwater cameras. You could see the glimmer in people's eyes when they were able to see the beauty of the ocean's ecosystem. When they learned what was at risk, it struck heart chords, and people signed up to volunteer time, or donate money for salmon research, rehabilitation, clean-up projects, and artificial reef installations (to provide habitat).

Events on a grassroots level that are connected to a global issue, such as greenhouse gas emissions, consumerism, or ocean pollution, are a great way to raise awareness and engage people who may not normally get involved in such topics. Events create an easy and simple way for a large group of people to take action and participate in something meaningful. Through these events, your community can engage with others around the world, to share ideas to make our communities greener and more integrated with our local and global ecology.

Look at the following list for opportunities to raise awareness, take action, or celebrate the environment (for more environmental dates, visit PlanetFriendly.net):

### World Water Day (March 22)

Supports conservation of clean, freshwater through promoting policy dialogue and awareness of the interlink between water and energy (http://www.unwater.org/worldwaterday).

**Action:** Host a roundtable meeting with local community stakeholders (e.g., government, schools, citizens, businesses, and industry) to discuss water issues and opportunities to create successful policies for water security.

### Earth Hour (Last Saturday in March)

Earth Hour started in 2007 as a lights-off event to raise awareness about climate change and energy conservation. It engages more than 150 countries worldwide. Earth Hour is typically on the Saturday of March, from 8:30 to 9:30 p.m. local time. Earth Hour can be successful through social media promotions and organizing gatherings (http://www.earthhour.org/).

## National Environmental Education Week (Mid-April)

Held primarily in the United States, National Environmental Education Week (EE Week) is a celebration of environmental education and it inspires environmental learning and stewardship among students. Local schools, colleges, and universities can register free online to participate in the event and get access to resources and funding opportunities (http://www.eeweek.org/).

## Earth Day (April 22)

Events worldwide are held to demonstrate support for protecting the environment. It was first celebrated in 1970, and is now hosted in almost 200 countries annually. Earth Day has been used as a platform for communities to announce new programs, policies, scholarships, and commitments to reducing environmental impact and moving forward as a progressive community. Earth Day is also celebrated to build awareness and take action on environmental causes that are salient to individual communities (http://www.earthday.org/).

**Action:** Rally people to clean a beach, remove invasive species, pick up litter from an environmentally sensitive area, plant trees, build a community garden, fundraise for a green energy project, show an environmental education movie in classrooms, organize a nature hike, or make recycled crafts.

## International Compost Awareness Week (First week of May)

International Compost Awareness Week (ICAW) is a comprehensive educational initiative featuring everything from composting in your backyard to large-scale consumer composting facilities. Your community can use this event as a platform for educating citizens and businesses about composting on a local level (http://compostingcouncil.org/icaw/).

**Action:** Compost education hour (a class on how to maintain a backyard compost), a tour of your local landfill, installing compost systems at local schools, or hosting a discussion about how to reduce waste in the community.

## International Day for Biological Diversity (May 22)

The United Nations proclaimed May 22 as International Day for Biological Diversity (IDB). Each year, there is a theme for IDB, such as "islands biodiversity" and "marine biodiversity." This event is a great way to get people talking about the vulnerabilities and value of local flora and fauna that may be at risk (http://www.cbd.int/idb/default.shtml).

### World Oceans Day (June 8)

World Oceans Day was originally proposed in 1992 by Canada at the Earth Summit in Rio de Janeiro, Brazil. It was officially recognized by the United Nations in 2008. Communities host educational events, beach cleans, fund-raisers, and celebrations for protecting the world's oceans (http://worldoceansday.org/).

### World Carfree Day (September 22)

World Carfree Day (WCD) was initiated to combat the North American car-dominated culture and showcase alternatives to driving such as walking, public transit, and bicycling (http://www.worldcarfree.net/wcfd/).

### Green Consumer Day (September 28)

Green Consumer Day is a relatively new initiative to raise awareness about consumption and the environmental impact of how and what we choose to buy. This day may seem like an oxymoron, if you believe consumption in itself is unsustainable; however, it can be a great way to point to green alternatives such as bringing your own shopping bag, buying organic, and reducing the amount of packaging that comes with products.

### International Volunteer Day (December 5)

International Volunteer Day (IVD) is a way to leverage volunteer activities to support important environmental or social causes. IVD was established by the United Nations in 1985. Since then, it has engaged organizations around the world to celebrate and thank volunteers, and organize special events that let people take action for an important global or a local cause (http://www.unv.org/what-we-do/intl-volunteer-day.html).

# 5
# *Using Green Transportation*

 Cities around the world recognize the impact of their transportation systems on the environment and on their communities as a whole. The North American suburban model of the 1950s and 1960s produced the most car-infused culture in the world. The environmental impacts of our transportation systems are well-documented, but keep this fact in mind, 21 countries in the world consume more than 1 million barrels of oil each day.[1]

How do you disconnect yourself from the oil addiction? Let's start by looking at steps for transitioning away from vehicles:

- **Consider the cost of vehicle ownership:** Is $5,000 a year important to you? Understanding the entire costs of owning a vehicle is an important first step that is explored in detail within this chapter. (see section 1.).

- **Consider all of the options:** A mix-and-match approach of multiple solutions will eventually lead you to question vehicle ownership altogether. Cycling, walking, transit, and several other ideas are discussed in section 2.

---

1 US Energy Information Administration (EIA), accessed March 2015.
http://www.eia.gov/countries/index.cfm?view=consumption

- **Drive greener:** Let's be honest, even those who ride their bike to work every day will likely still own a vehicle, and this doesn't excuse them from driving in the evening and weekends. Everyone can find ways to drive greener and at the same time reduce some of the costs of ownership (see section 3.).

## 1. The Cost of Vehicle Ownership

We must begin with understanding the true impacts and cost of a vehicle before we can discuss the range of alternatives. First, the car has always been a symbol of personal freedom in North America. Unfortunately, our obsession with the car resulted in it being the priority for city planning as well.

Secondly, the environmental impact of vehicles is unmatched when it comes to our individual carbon footprints. For most people, emissions from their vehicles are twice that of their homes. In the core of cities, emissions are normally balanced between vehicles and buildings, but in the large suburbs that surround the cities, vehicles represent 60 to 70 percent of the total community emissions.

More recently, younger generations are entering adulthood with a completely different perspective. Why do I need or want a vehicle? The financial savings and flexibility of not owning a vehicle has become very appealing and car companies know it. Young North Americans cannot justify the expense and effort of becoming a vehicle owner. Cost alone is a primary motivator, thanks to the increase of insurance, fuel, maintenance, and repair.

Consumer Reports conducted a review of average car costs, and found that the lowest cost of ownership per year, over the first 5 years, is $5,000 for the Toyota Prius C.[2] TravelSmart put the annual cost of ownership as more than $10,000 per year.[3] If you considered the range of alternatives to owning a vehicle and the potential costs, you will find that you can use a combination of transportation alternatives and pay a lot less. For example, taking a taxi once a week ($1,000), an annual bus pass ($1,000), car-share membership ($500), and your bike, would cover your transportation needs for half the price every year.

Assess the costs of vehicle ownership versus the alternatives that are available to you (see Diagram 2). Focus on your daily commute; by doing so, you have the best chance of changing your behavior as this is the opportunity to establish a consistent pattern in your daily

2  "What That Car Really Costs to Own," Consumer Reports, accessed February 2015.
   http://consumerreports.org/cro/2012/12/what-that-car-really-costs-to-own/index.htm
3  "Carpool Survey Results Are In," TravelSmart, accessed February 2015.
   http://www.travelsmart.ca/en/GVRD/Carpooling/Carpool-Survey-Results-3.aspx

routine. Leaving the car behind and choosing greener commute alternatives should be considered an important accomplishment for anyone.

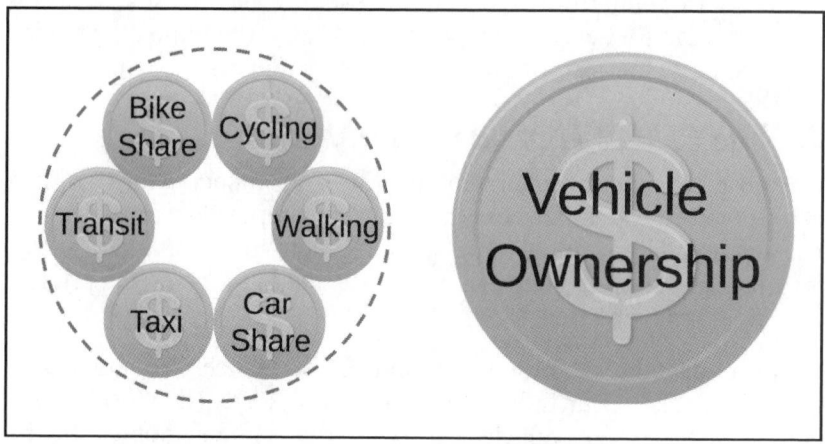

Diagram 2: Green Alternatives versus Vehicle Ownership

## 2. Transportation Alternatives

Look around and you will find some neat tools available to discover the best and fastest way to commute and perhaps help you choose the most transportation-friendly place to live.

Google (maps.google.com) has expanded it mapping features to the level of being a daily transportation planner, providing you with time lines for all modes of transportation (e.g., walking, cycling, transit, and driving). Zoom in to check out the condition of roads and trails and see where congestion and construction is happening in town at the same time.

While we are talking about going online, online shopping is another tool to consider that lets someone else do the driving. The benefit comes from the delivery of goods that involve multiple stops, allowing the service to be environmentally and fiscally efficient. Although we want you to support your local economy, purchases you would make at a mall can be avoided by shopping online. The prices can be less expensive, the delivery is fast, and you don't need a car to get there. You can still support your local economy through your regular daily purchases such as groceries and other supplies.

What if food-delivery service became more commonplace? Food-delivery services have already been regularly provided at a premium for seniors but now new companies are delivering local fresh food to directly to your door. The urban delivery of local produce has been expanded by companies such as Sustainable Produce Urban Delivery (SPUD) which focuses on providing sustainable, local food to everyone. Plus, one truck making ten deliveries produces less emission than ten car trips to the store.

For people who are looking to avoid purchasing a vehicle, or limit its use, the following sections include considerations and alternatives for you to ponder.

## 2.1 Bicycling

The bicycle is a powerful symbol these days and has become much more than solely an alternative transportation option. Its simplicity and independence is revered, to the point that passionate cyclists can be intimidating to others and this has helped to create several subcultures within the cycling community itself. Human-powered freedom is greatly desired by many, but the cycling infrastructure of your community greatly influences people's decisions to bike on a regular basis.

The bicycle is an icon of the green city, and those who strive to be the greenest cities in the world (e.g., Vancouver, Copenhagen, Portland) put cycling infrastructure at the forefront of their initiatives. They are moving the bar beyond painted stripe bike lanes, to dedicated and protected lanes. Cycling can no longer be considered just a fad, as cycling rates have significantly increased across many cities in the US and Canada since 1990.[4]

However, unless you live in a progressive cycling city, finding room for your bike amongst most current road designs can be downright dangerous. Road transformation to accommodate cycling is starting in urban areas and it will take time and money to implement this level of cycling infrastructure into the suburban environment. For example, Greater Victoria in BC has taken advantage of an old railway bed to establish one of the best continuous bike trail systems in an urban environment. Now the challenge is for municipalities to build off this gem to link their residents between their homes, offices, and schools.

Things you can do to improve your chances of cycling:

- Study your optimal route and find where the best cycling routes are: Most cities now have maps available to show you the various locations of cycling routes in your community. We are always hopeful that there will be logical, clearly marked routes

---

4 "In 1990, Seattle Topped Portland and Nearly Every Other City in Bike Commuting," Seattle, Bike Blog, accessed March 2015. http://www.seattlebikeblog.com/2013/06/25/in-1990-seattle-topped-portland-and-nearly-every-other-us-city-in-bike-commuting/

waiting for us, but the truth is that bike lanes will start and stop in strange locations in your community. There are many reasons for this, and a common one is that one particular development creates a block of ideal cycling lanes in the middle of a cycling wasteland. The hope is that eventually the community will connect these lanes to other routes, but again, time and money.

- Get the right equipment: Set yourself up for success with the right bike, proper reflective gear, front and rear lights and rear-view mirrors. The right helmet and lock are also essential.

- Learn how to fix a bike yourself: Take a bike course that will teach you the basics of maintenance and repair, and you will be prepared for 90 percent of the breakdowns you may face.

- Respect the car: Although we want drivers to take care around cyclists, it is not in your best interest to make assumption about moving vehicles. Unless you are built like a truck, you will always lose that battle. Follow the rules of the road like a vehicle would and you will greatly reduce your chances of getting in an accident.

- Bike with a friend: Improve your chances of staying committed to cycling to work or school by cycling with a friend. Making it fun and social helps the ride breeze by.

To enhance the cycling system in your community, small advances can make a big difference. You can work alongside your local municipality, or with public areas such as schools, community centers, and major destinations such as airports and job sites to improve conditions for cycling. Here are a few ideas:

1. Set up a bicycle repair zone: Often called a "Bike Kitchen," these are stations along popular bike trails or destinations that have a bicycle stand, pump, and repair tools that riders can use for free.

2. Install covered bike parking: Covered bicycle racks, with motion-sensor lights that activate during dark hours, can help reduce bicycle theft and keep a rider's bike dry. It's a small improvement, but for a rider, it creates a better experience. The visual aspect is important too because having quality, secure bike storage is a signal to the community that the town values cycling and cyclists.

3. Start a bicycle bursary program: SPOKES is a successful bicycle bursary program at the University of Victoria that takes in worn out or underused bicycles, donated from the community, and fixes them. These refurbished bikes are then loaned on an annual basis to students at the university who can't afford to purchase a bike.

4. Start a bicycle sharing program: Bike sharing started in Europe, but these public programs are now popular in China, New York, and many other places. Some require a deposit or membership in order to "borrow" bicycles and most have stations throughout the city where they can be parked, allowing people to grab a bike and travel from point A to point B without having to return it to point A.

5. Promote bike to work week: This event is popular around the world and is a great way to get people, who haven't biked to work before, to give it a try. Often, people will become comfortable with the route, enjoy the ride, and start to commute via bicycle more often.

## 2.2 Walking

Cities that are good to walk in are simply better places to live. Walking isn't just about commuting in a manner that reduces fossil fuels; it's about human connection, good health, and creating a desirable place to live.

Street design has a big impact on the health of a community. If the streets are not designed for walking, biking, and human interaction, they will not foster those behaviors. The city will feel cold and individuals will feel deprived of community and isolated. City design is important for the life of every citizen, so get engaged with your local municipality and give feedback into what your streets could be, and how they shape how we live. For more resources on this topic, visit www.walklive.org.

The renewed interest in the walkability of a city has resulted in a unique online tool, Walk Score (www.walkscore.com). Walk Score is a tool that started as a small project and then expanded into a planning tool used by people ranging from realtors to apartment hunters. Type in an address and a plethora of information is provided including a descriptive walk score and transit score, a description of the location, and an excellent travel-time map that shows the range of transport by different modes based on the time parameters you set. Variations of this concept are also available such as TravelSmart in Vancouver, BC, which looks to further help people make better travel choices by providing additional tips.

## 2.3 Car- and bike-sharing programs

Car-sharing used to be a small, localized affair, but technology has allowed new services to emerge. Traditional car-share models require the cars to be returned back to their original locations, but new systems are allowing users to drop off cars where it is convenient for them.

Car2Go was originally a German idea by Daimler AG, which allowed users to rent vehicles for one-way use and charged them for use by the minute. This service in now available in 17 cities in North America, with the city of Vancouver having the greatest uptake of 750 vehicles available to users. Only Hamburg and Vienna surpass the popularity of the vehicles in Vancouver.

Bike shares have also emerged; for example, Bixi (bixi.com) is a nonprofit and public bicycle-sharing system that was developed in Montreal and implemented in 2008. Bixi has now expanded across the US, most prominently in New York (6,000 bikes), and into Europe, most notably in London (9,200 bikes). The bikes have docking stations distributed throughout participating cities, making it easy to take a bike and drop it off at another location.

## 3. Drive Greener

We know the transition away from the vehicle won't be possible for some for a variety of reasons, so how can you drive greener? Here are some steps you can take when you drive your vehicle:

- Drive less in general by considering your need to drive each time.
- Drive better to reduce emissions, by reducing your acceleration and your overall speed.
- Multitask your trips to make the most of your outing.
- Keep your vehicle in good condition, such as regular tune-ups and checking and filling the tires.
- Avoid idling whenever possible.
- Drive to transit or subway if it is not easily accessible to you.
- Consider the purchase of an electric vehicle or low-emissions vehicle.

## 3.1  Electric vehicles

While cycling advocates will cringe at the thought of supporting vehicles on the road, the truth is that most everyone appreciates the benefits of a vehicle. We must also acknowledge that many people simply will never give up that convenience and comfort so encouraging the use of electric vehicles is a good way to get people to go green.

Many electric vehicle (EV) drivers find it is more fun to drive than regular gas or diesel vehicle! The acceleration of EVs is so impressive that they have now set a new record for the famous 0-60 miles per hour measure of vehicle supremacy. Let's also be honest about existing concerns about EVs:

- Cost.

- Battery life.

- Appropriately coined term "range anxiety."

The cost of EVs is currently about $10,000 more than an equivalent-sized gasoline car, but in many areas incentives are being provided by government agencies to increase the uptake. These range from $5,000 to $8,500, but incentives alone should not be your only consideration and these additional savings quickly remove the financial barrier.

First, the simplicity of an EV greatly reduces the maintenance costs. The gas vehicle has an internal-combustion engine that is a complex system of parts that continuously requires replacement of engine parts and fluids to function.

Secondly, there is the cost of electricity compared to gas. Depending on where you live, you will be paying 70 to 90 percent less on fuel per mile, because of the relatively low cost of electricity. Depending on how much you drive, this can mean savings of $1,000 to $2,000 per year.

The life of an EV battery is one issue that has not be fully tested because of how new EVs are to the market. Many are concerned about what that replacement cost will be but this concern should be reduced by the five-year battery warranty that is now coming with new vehicles. However, the prominent EV maker, Tesla, is constructing a new battery "gigafactory" which will help mass produce EVs.

Some will argue that the electricity used in the cars still comes from high-carbon sources in many jurisdictions. However, in this challenge lies an opportunity to switch to low-carbon sources of electricity, one that is not available with the internal-combustion engine of a gas-using vehicle. Solar panels at your home can produce the equivalent energy you need to power an EV. Imagine being able to claim your car is solar powered!

The best way for you to determine whether an EV is right for you is to drive one first. Try one at a dealership and ask questions. Then, find out from others in the community and see what their experiences are. This will help you determine how comfortable you will be with making the jump to an electric vehicle.

Lastly, check out the website PlugShare.com, which will help provide a cure for the most serious of electric vehicle affliction, range anxiety. Plug Share is the prominent resource for electric vehicles charging stations in North America. Need that comfort of knowing that a charging station is nearby? You will be shocked to see how many charging stations are located in your community. The interactive map provides detailed information for each charging location including charging type (slow, medium, or fast charging), status of the stations (occupied or service status), and feedback from other users about that particular station.

However, what many EV owners are finding is that they don't rely on these stations as much as expected. It is great to have them available if needed, but if you plug in your vehicle at home each night, you will start each day with a full charge. That is a convenient benefit of the EV.

# 6
# *Foundations of a Green Home*

A green community starts with a green home. Your values guide you to the type of place you want to live, and the root of this is how you live at home. Your home is your place of rest, nourishment, and safekeeping. It should make you feel peaceful and have room for creative thought. A sustainable home provides for those who dwell in it, without compromising needs of future generations by taking and wasting too much. A green home can be an inspiration to a whole community, and start to change a neighborhood's identify.

Your home plays a role in defining your community. It's a place of demonstration, where you can try new techniques, such as capturing rain water with a rain-barrel system, planting a food garden, or get your own backyard chickens. When people see others taking innovative steps to reduce environmental impact, they start asking questions — sometimes with skepticism, sometimes with awe. Install a solar panel system and you might have to start providing tours! I have seen families and individuals start to re-create their home environment based on their own commitment to sustainable living and the finished products drew much attention. Many people are intrigued by the idea of an efficient, zero-waste, resourceful home, but don't know where to start. Your home can be a beacon and an example for how whole communities can become more sustainable.

In this chapter we discuss the footprint of your home. Your actions have power that can set an example for others, so be ready to share. To understand the environmental footprint of your home, consider where your home is located, what types of mechanical systems operate your home, the envelope components, how you utilize your outdoor space, and how you operate within it.

## 1. Home Size and Location

Let's start with some key up-front decisions that most impacts how green your home is. Where you decide to live dictates what your carbon footprint is in two ways:

1. Your home's location in the community.

2. Your home's size.

What influences your decisions in where you want to live? About 40 years ago, the city was seen as a place for work and entertainment, but not a place to live. The focus on the suburbs ended up being one of the biggest sustainability mistakes of the last 100 years because of the reliance on vehicles and the ability to build very large homes. However, something has changed over the last ten years, as a focus has returned to making the city a desirable place for people of all ages.

Making life close to the city better means that we are not as dispersed and the opportunities for alternative and active transportation options improves. Living closer to work and school means you will be more likely to ride a bicycle, take the bus, or walk as part of your daily commute.

The second key factor goes against traditional expectations. The recognition that "small can be beautiful" is a new concept to North Americans (maybe not if you live in New York) and has been a necessity for major cities around the world for years. Development of the suburbs into the land surrounding major centers allowed for larger homes to be built at a lower cost. These days, people are looking at smaller homes for affordability, less work (cleaning), and to reduce their environmental footprint. Less space forces you to think twice about your purchases and, when you look to sell, a smaller, more affordable home is more likely to sell faster.

How to live in a smaller space more efficiently:

- Using built-in bookcases that are a part of the wall.

- Maximizing storage space under stairs, bed frames, and bench seating.

- Install modular and multiuse systems such as upholstered cubes that can act as extra seating, coffee tables, or footstools, and Murphy beds that can fold into the wall with a pull down dining table underneath.

- Extending cabinets and bookshelves to the ceiling.

- Hanging racks for pots and pans in the kitchen.

---

### A Tiny Home for a Big Future

A young couple from Victoria, BC had big dreams. They both loved Mexico and surfing. They wanted to have a property on the Baja where they could spend winter months eating tacos de pescado and riding the big waves. Their life in Victoria was pleasant, with a house in a nice area and lots of friends in their lives. However, even though they both worked full time, the reality of buying the land and building a house in Mexico was far from reach with their current spending on rent and utilities.

To take matters into their own hands, the couple did the math. Rent was costing them big bucks, and the solution was to entirely change how they lived. They decided to build a tiny home on a mobile flat deck, completely self-sufficient with solar power, a composting toilet, and propane stove and fridge. This small space would be well-designed yet compact, and the best part: After a few years of living in the tiny home, the building expenses would be paid off within the first year, and in three years they would be able to buy their dream lot on the Baja.

This move did not come without sacrifice. They had to reduce their possessions. There was nowhere to fit 30 pairs of shoes, or even more than a few sets of dishes. Everything in the space had to be useful and important. This couple broke the class equation of rent, rent, rent, and, eventually, buy. Instead, they changed their lifestyle in order to pursue their dreams. In the meantime, they found a way to live with a small environmental footprint, and reduced their reliance on the standard service grid as well as their possessions.

---

## 2. Evaluating Your Home

What does it mean to "build green"? It depends on how you want to define it. There are many certifications available that provide a range of definitions for a variety of building types. It can be overwhelming to understand the different certifications without the help of a professional. The reason for this is that the rating systems include such a comprehensive list of green features for consideration. So it is important to remember that building green can also be a more modest process. Some people are focusing on energy, by achieving the highest possible energy rating for their homes and reducing their carbon footprints the most.

The most prominent new residential home building certifications include Leadership in Energy and Environmental Design (LEED) and Built Green. There are some common threads within these certifications:

- Energy use ratings.

- Overall water use.

- Building materials.

- Indoor air quality.

- Transportation options.

Most certifications make energy consumption the priority. The "Passivhaus" (i.e., passive house) originated in Germany, a concept that focuses on achieving very low energy consumption by maximizing wall thickness and solar orientation. We explore this concept further in Chapter 8.

The best option is to meet with several architects who have built green homes in your area and see what they have to say. Make sure to also look into any local building requirements that may impact your green dream home.

To support further uptake of green building practices in your community, get engaged with your local green building association. LEED certifications are overseen by the US Green Building Council (USGBC) and by the Canada Green Building Council (CaGBC). These organizations are supported by local chapters that regularly look to engage with the local building community, local governments, and residents. This is a great way for you to connect with the latest green building practices.

For more information about renovating your home see *Greening Your Home: Successful Eco-Renovation Strategies*, another book in the Self-Counsel Press *Green Series*.

For those of you who are not ready to build a new green home, you may be looking for improvements you can make to your existing home. The truth is that the best energy savings are the same things that home owners have been hearing for 40 years. Your building envelope is what contains the temperature level of your home, and in most homes, air conditioning and heating are major energy users. Yes, insulation and windows are still king when it comes to saving energy in your home!

A professional audit will provide you with a detailed report about where you will get the most energy savings for your dollar such as the heating system, windows, insulation, or a combination of them all. Before you get a professional energy advisor to review your home, a good starting point is to access the EPA's free Energy Star Home Energy Yardstick tool.[1] This simple assessment will provide your home's annual energy use compared to similar homes in your area. (Some Canadian utilities such as BC Hydro also provide this service.) These might not provide all the details you want, but they will be able to give you a sense of where to start with your renovations.

There is also a useful Do-It-Yourself Home Energy Audit, created by the Vancouver Green Capital, that is available to download.[2] Not all of the information may apply to your region, so check for local resources in your area.

If you are looking for a quick energy audit of your home, there are basic questions that an energy auditor asks and the answers will give you an idea of where you stand:

- **How old is your home?** Construction standards have evolved (e.g., newspaper insulation in a 100-year-old home) so the older your home is, the less energy efficient it will be.

- **What type of heating system do you have?** We cover this discussion thoroughly in section 2.1 on heating systems.

- **What type of windows do you have and how old are they?** Considerations include the type of windows (e.g., single pane and double pane) and how old they are. The optimal window

---

1 "Energy Star Home Energy Yardstick," Environmental Protection Agency (EPA), accessed February 2015. https://www.energystar.gov/index.cfm?fuseaction=home_energy_yardstick.showgetstarted
2 "Do-It-Yourself Home Energy Audit," Vancouver Green Capital, accessed February 2015. http://vancouver.ca/files/cov/green-energy-audit-guide.pdf

is a triple-pane that is used in the most energy-efficient homes such a passive homes.

- **How much insulation is in your attic and walls?** Insulation is measured by something called the R-value or RSI value. Estimates can be made for your R-value or RSI value based on its thickness. You can calculate the R-value of your attic insulation by multiplying the thickness of your insulation by a factor based on the type of insulation you have in the attic. For example, if your home has cellulose insulation at a depth of 8 inches between the joists, the attic insulation has an R-value of 3.7 times 8, or 29.6. Depending on where you live, a good level of insulation is considered to be between R-30 and R-50.

- **Can you identify the source of air leaks in your home?** The source of air leaks in your home can be found in the usual places such as doors, windowsills, and fireplace dampers. There are also some sneaky places such as behind light switches, plug outlets, and baseboards. You can buy sensors to help find these leaks, or you can conduct your own pressurization test by using the following steps from Energy.Gov's to identify leaks:[3]

  - Turn off all combustion appliances such as gas burning furnaces and water heaters on a cool, very windy day.

  - Shut all windows, exterior doors, and fireplace flues.

  - Turn on all exhaust fans that blow air outside, such as your clothes dryer, bathroom fans, or stove vents, or use a large window fan to suck out the air in the rooms.

  - Light an incense stick and pass it around the edges of common leak sites. Wherever the smoke wavers or is sucked out of or blown into the room, there's a draft. You can also use a damp hand to locate leaks; any drafts will feel cool to your hand.

## 2.1 Heating your home

The greenhouse gas emissions and natural environment impacts stemming from you home heating can vary not only by fuel type (i.e., electricity or gas) but can also depend on how electricity is generated in your particular part of the world. Of course, you need to find a balance between the environmental impact of your home heating system and the costs. So what it the right balance for you?

---

3 "Detecting Air Leaks," Energy.gov, accessed February 2015.
   http://www.energy.gov/energysaver/articles/detecting-air-leaks]

So let's help you understand you're heating system better by reviewing the different systems, their environmental impacts, and the cost of energy in your area. Changes to your home heating system are never simple, but the more you understand your system the better short- and long-term choices you can make. Let's explore some of the systems:

- **Electric baseboard:** This is the heating equivalent to the incandescent lightbulb; electric baseboards provide a simple, albeit inefficient, heat source that is possible in almost all geographic locations. They are low maintenance and can function for more than 20 years.

- **Furnace (e.g., natural gas, heating oil, or electric):** Warm air from either the burning of natural gas or heating oil, or a heated electric coil, is distributed through ducts into the home. These different types of fuels have very different greenhouse gas emissions and costs to consider.

- **Radiant heating:** Uses a boiler to heat up water which is then distributed throughout a building via radiators. This is also known as hydronic heating, where boilers commonly use gas or oil as a fuel source. While the radiator system has become less common, there is renewed interest in hydronic heat because of its potential to connect to district energy systems.

- **Air source heat pump:** Think about the same technology that is used in your refrigerator, just used in reverse for home heating. Advancements in the technology have made heat pumps an energy-efficient and low-carbon option for heating and cooling homes. They are prominent in areas where cooling is also needed in the summer. Heat pumps also use significantly less energy to provide heat when compared to baseboards and furnaces.

Which heating system is right for you? You still need some more information before you can make your decision. What is the greenest more cost-effective option? The heat pump will often stand out as the best environmental decision, as long as you are OK with paying more up front.

How about the ultimate home heating option? If you install solar panels to power your heat pump, you are looking at a very sustainable way of heating your home.

Across North America, electricity is generated in different ways usually due to geography. In US states such as Washington, Oregon, and California; and Canadian provinces such as British Columbia and Quebec, mountains and sunshine provide the opportunity for low-carbon electricity from hydroelectric dams and solar panels. These dams do have an enormous environmental footprint when they are first built, often resulting in the flooding of valuable natural spaces and fertile farmland. After that, however, they produce energy with an extremely low-carbon footprint and the extended life span of the dams means they don't need to be replaced.

For most other regions, electricity is generated through the burning of fossil fuels in the form of coal, oil, or natural gas. This produces a significantly higher carbon footprint and these fuels are associated with environmental impacts during their extraction and shipment.

You generate greenhouse gas emissions from burning fuel when you drive, burning oil, or gas for home heating, or using electricity generated from coal, natural gas, oil, and even hydro dams. Greenhouse gas emissions will vary depending on your area and personal behaviors. Calculating your carbon footprint will be a valuable exercise for you as you will learn where you can make the biggest impact to reduce it. Depending on where you live, try out one of the calculators and see how you can make a difference:

- US calculator: http://www.epa.gov/climatechange/ ghgemissions individual.html

- US and Canada calculator: http://www.carbonfootprint.com/ calculator1.html

You can monitor your home's energy consumption by using a home-energy monitor, which takes a reading from your meter if you are in an area where smart meters have been enabled. Smart meters are updated versions of the energy-measurement tools used by electrical utilities to measure your household energy consumption. These monitors will provide more than a simple energy-consumption reading. Newer monitors are providing costs and time-of-day data that will help you focus on your most energy-consuming lights, gadgets, and appliances. Check your local utility provider's website for more information or you may find a monitor at your local electronics store.

## 2.2 Electronics, appliances, and lights

This is an area that home owners and renters of all building types can take action. Buying the right items for you home can make a big difference in your energy consumption. The Environmental Protection Agency (EPA) developed a program called Energy Star, which has greatly improved the efficiency of energy-consuming items in the home. This is a voluntary program for businesses, but has become a standard the electronics, appliance, and lighting industries have embraced.

The program helps businesses and individuals save money and protect the climate through superior energy efficiency. If you want to just focus on some key items, think about the big energy consumers in your house and when you are in need of a new dishwasher, stove or washer/dryer, look for Energy Star labeling.

LED lights have evolved to become the best energy-saving technology over the last five years and their performance continues to advance each year, even as the price goes down. Household LED bulbs are currently producing the equivalent of 60-watt and 100-watt lighting while only using 10 to 12 watts of power. For most users, this means you are paying off the bulb within a year and the bulb lasts 20!

## 3. Living Green in an Apartment or Condo

"Multifamily building owners and tenants spent nearly $22 billion on energy in 2009, an average of $1,141 per household. If the best current multifamily energy-efficiency programs were expanded nationwide, they could save owners and tenants up to $3.4 billion per year."[4]

Living in an apartment or condo presents different challenges when it comes to green living. Shared facilities and the need to mobilize other people (i.e., tenants, property managers, strata council, landlords) can create roadblocks to making a difference in your building as a whole.

Unlike single-family homes, creating the business case for greening an apartment can be challenging. With triple-net lease agreements, the building operating costs are included in the rent, and often the renters don't pay or even see the energy, water, and gas bills for their unit. Thus, renters have no cost incentive to invest in energy improvements or change their behaviors. Similarly, if tenants do pay their own utility bill, a landlord will have no incentive to invest in the tenants' space in order to reduce their energy bills. The high turnover in some buildings also creates a disincentive because investments in energy efficiency may not pay back for a longer period of time than the lease or ownership of the unit.

Despite all these challenges, there is a lot of room for improvement in multifamily housing efficiency, and models for shared benefit for both landlords and tenants.

4 "Engaging as Partners: Introducing Utilities to the Energy Efficiency Needs of Multifamily Buildings and Their Owners," Anne McKibbin, CNT Energy, American Council for an Energy-Efficient Economy, accessed March 2015. http://aceee.org/research-report/e137

When I ask people about greening their apartment building, I often hear responses along the lines of "Oh, they will *never* go for that," or "Yeah, I would like to, but my strata council is so old school and stuffy," or "My landlord simply doesn't care."

The best advice we can give is to speak from a place of shared benefit, rather than personal values. Here is the difference:

Option A: "We should be composting, saving energy, and installing bike racks because climate change will cause the seas to rise and we will all be heading for the hills if we don't do something about it. In addition, if we don't do this, the polar bears will die. Did I mention that not doing this makes you bad people?"

You may get some deer-in-headlights looks in response. Option B is a better way to go about it:

Option B: "Our building manager and owners are looking for ways to save money. I think we can save some money by focusing on reducing our environmental impact. Not all upgrades save money, but some have great savings and could fund other upgrades. For example, lighting motion sensors are inexpensive to install and will start saving money within a few months. As our energy bills go down, our building can pay for a composting system that will reduce our trash and make the tenants feel good about being in a green building."

The Option B discourse can help you start on the right foot with your building manager, strata council, or landlord when you are working to green your building.

Compared to the single-family housing market, multifamily buildings have been left out of many of the programs, incentives, and innovations that have been taking place in buildings management and construction. This size of building has been flagged as a major opportunity by many building science experts, waiting for action and leadership. The question of leadership is a tough one, as there are many groups and individuals with different interests and priorities involved in multiunit residential buildings.

Though there are far fewer case studies of multifamily residential than individual homes, a few buildings have taken great strides towards fostering sustainable and healthy living.

In Ontario, a program called Living Green Together began in 2014 by the Federation of Rental Housing Providers of Ontario. The program offers ten standards in addition to its existing Certified Rental

Building Program. These standards work to build an environmentally conscious culture within the buildings, connecting renters, property owners and managers.

Your community can connect with the landlord and property-management industry by introducing programs, incentives, and best practices for greening buildings, outlining the benefits for both renters and property owners or managers.

## 4. Daily Practices Make a Difference

The most common challenge sustainability practitioners understand, you can build a green home or buy a green product, but it will be a waste of money if the occupants and operators are not properly operating and "green misbehaving" in the home. For example, you can buy an energy-efficient dishwasher, but if it is only half full when you run it, it will cost you a lot more in the end. Put simply, it comes down to the daily practices that will dictate how green your home is. Here is a snapshot of other green behaviors in your home that you should make a regular part of your life:

- Install programmable thermostats, which automatically lower temperature when asleep or away from the house.
- Use dimmers on lights.
- Unplug electronics during extended absences.
- Use a clothesline or drying rack instead of a dryer.
- Reduce heating in rooms that aren't used often.
- Close the curtains on hot days.
- Use cold water when possible for washing clothes.
- Turn up your refrigerator so that you are not cooling more than you have too.
- Turn down your water heater thermostat.
- Use low-flow showerheads.
- Lower the temperature during hours when you are asleep.
- Dress warmer instead of increasing the temperature in your home.
- If you live in a condo or apartment, put up information posters on energy saving and other green practices that most apply.

# 7
# *Water Systems*

*Definition of "water security": "The capacity of a population to safeguard sustainable access to adequate quantities of acceptable quality water for sustaining livelihoods, human well-being, and socio-economic development, for ensuring protection against water-borne pollution and water-related disasters, and for preserving ecosystems in a climate of peace and political stability."*

— UN-Water Analytical Brief on Water Security and the
Global Water Agenda, 2013

 Most North Americans have easy access to water, straight from the tap. This convenience makes water seem abundantly available, but the truth is freshwater systems of our world are in great danger. Water is essential for all life on the planet. Of all of the water on Earth, three percent is freshwater, which mostly still remains in glaciers and ice caps. The precious, small amount of freshwater usable to humankind is located underground and in rivers and lakes.

Our activities have abused clean water resources with pollution and overuse. Even in rain forest areas, studies are showing that freshwater reserves are at risk of drying up, meaning that water is being taken at a rate far greater than it can naturally replenish.

In communities where freshwater sources have run dry or become too polluted, they have resorted to removing the salt from saltwater. This desalination process is intense and very expensive. There can also be adverse effects on marine ecosystems with the discharge of highly concentrated brine back into the ocean.[1]

Other communities have polluted downstream ecosystems with sewage effluent, agricultural chemicals, and toxins, turning what were pristine, life-supporting habitats into dead-zone sludge.

For sustainability and resilience, we need to protect our freshwater systems and recognize the connectivity of the world water system. Despite their importance, freshwater systems are declining faster than terrestrial systems, and the extinction rate of freshwater species coincides with this decline.[2] Some of the major threats include the creation of dams, drainage of marshes and wetlands, pollution from dumping, agricultural runoff, overuse of groundwater, invasive species, and changing flow patterns.

While many systems are in a state of peril, there are both local and global initiatives working to help communities protect, rehabilitate, and detoxify freshwater systems. As awareness grows and our communities take action, it is incredible to see how the waterways bounce back from a state of doom. It is possible to see a polluted stream full of fish and murky lakes become clear once again. Nature will find a way, if we cooperate. Nature is designed to be resilient.

We can begin by making changes to protect freshwater for humankind and other species. Reducing water usage, finding alternatives to pesticides and chemicals in agriculture, and protecting wetland areas are just a few examples. Many communities have established public interest groups formed to preserve and protect these areas. If you don't have one, you may consider starting a group and bringing together citizens, government, and businesses to find solutions. The majority of water we use in the world is not recaptured or treated. We can find hundreds of ways to make better use of the water we consume and leave it in a better state when we return it to the natural world.

1 "Key Issues in Seawater Desalination in California: Marine Impacts." Heather Cooley, Newsha Ajami, and Mathew Heberger, Pacific Institute, accessed March 2015. http://pacinst.org/wp-content/uploads/sites/21/2013/12/desal-marine-imapcts-full-report.pdf
2 "Inland Waters Biodiversity," Convention on Biological Diversity, accessed March 2015. http://www.cbd.int/undb/media/factsheets/undb-factsheet-waters-en.pdf

Water security and human well-being are inextricably linked. Vast population, even entire nations, lack availability to clean and healthy drinking water. This impacts not only their health, but their ability to grow food, treat illness, and gain access to other regions.

# 1. Watershed Areas

Watersheds are areas that catch precipitation and channel it into lakes and streams. This water feeds into groundwaters, providing important sources of drinking water. Streams, rivers, lakes, and water networks may form a watershed area, which varies with topography. These areas are important because they directly impact water quality. For this reason, water-conservation efforts often focus on watersheds.

If pesticides are used in areas within the watershed, they are likely entering the water. When it rains, water flows over and through the land, carrying nutrients and providing the area with life-giving clean water. The concern is that these watersheds are overused for activities such as irrigation, and polluted by motor oil, heavy metals, and other contaminants.

Keeping our water clean is critical for the health of our communities and wildlife. Watersheds give us a tangible scope for working on water use and contamination issues, but we must remember that water systems are all connected; none exist as isolated bodies or conduits. A polluted lake can impact an entire groundwater network, streams, and downstream ecosystems. It is important that efforts to conserve and protect water resources occur congruently on local, regional, and international levels.

Ultimately, sustainability of water means that we do not pollute our water systems or drain them at a rate that cannot be replenished. Water security is inextricably linked to social justice. Taking and polluting water in one area will undoubtedly impact another community. Water areas have cultural history, and the means of supplying populations with food, water, and economic sustenance. Even today, it is estimated that 1 billion people do not have access to clean drinking water. Protecting watersheds isn't just about preserving natural ecosystems, it's about providing for our communities and our neighbors.

---

### The Story of the Colorado River

The Colorado River is 1,450 miles (2,330 kilometers) long and one of the biggest rivers in the United States. Many watershed areas flow into the Colorado River; it flows southwest from the Rocky Mountains through the states and into Mexico. Historically, a powerful river that carved the Grand Canyon, it once emptied into the Gulf of California. Now, this overused river no longer reaches the sea.

The Colorado River runs dry, no longer reaching its delta area in most years (i.e., a delta is an area where a river meets the sea). These areas are important breeding and feeding grounds, often rich in biodiversity and populations of birds, spawning fish, and unique plants. The Colorado River is an important water source for irrigation, and power source for nearby communities. It has dams along its route in the southern states and the water is extracted in huge volumes for farm land, which has devastating repercussions on the Mexican-delta region that relied on the river meeting the sea to sustain migratory species, such as shrimp and the native Cocopah (the People of the River)[3] Agricultural runoff has resulted in high contaminant levels in the lower river area.[4]

Efforts to restore the Colorado and prevent continued damage have been ongoing for decades, with varying degrees of success. Many damming projects were stopped due to concerned citizen groups. Other organizations today, such as Save the Colorado (http://savethecolorado.org/) are promoting solutions such as water recycling and reuse, water efficiency in households, community planning (i.e., policies that support water conservation), removing dams that are no longer useful, and establishing water-sharing agreements with farmers. There is hope for the Colorado if citizens, academia, local government, and industry work together.

# 2. Water Use in Our Communities

At the community level, conservation initiatives through partnerships among urban water agencies, public interest organizations, and private entities have been very successful. Every community has a unique water-use profile — like a fingerprint — of how it accesses and uses water. For this reason, it is important for each community to consider its specific needs for water use, collect data, and set targets based on

---

3 "Where the Colorado Runs Dry," Jonathan Waterman, *The New York Times* (February 14, 2012), accessed February 2015. http://www.nytimes.com/2012/02/15/opinion/where-the-colorado-river-runs-dry.html?_r=0

4 "Technical Report: Pesticides in the Lower Colorado River," Surveillance and Analysis Division (Report No. 002<\#150>73, April 1973), United States Environmental Protection Agency, accessed February 2015. http://cfpub.epa.gov/ols/catalog/advanced_full_record.cfm?&FIELD1=SUBJECT&INPUT1=Conditions&TYPE1=EXACT&LOGIC1=AND&COLL=&SORT_TYPE=MTIC&item_count=1178&item_accn=384378

both the needs of future populations, business activity, and ecological needs. A strong community water-conservation plan will consider the linkages between drinking water, wastewater types, sewage, and rainwater.

Water is a challenging topic for planners because it is a flowing, changing resource. A systems approach is required to understand how we as humans can change how we build our cities, treat water, manage its flow, and what we put in it. To be effective in sustainable water planning, we must consider how water is extracted, filtered, treated, heated, used, discharged, wasted, and recycled. Water is also linked to how we use energy. It takes a lot of energy to heat water, which we use both in businesses and homes. Water conservation inherently means energy conservation, which is an added bonus. A reduction in energy consumption reduces greenhouse gas emissions. Therefore, water conservation is important for addressing climate change.

There are also social and cultural considerations. Water offers an abundance of fish and other animals. It provides for livelihoods and enjoyment. Humans have naturally settled close to water sources, and many of these areas are important to our culture and history.

Conservation is a multiyear, long-term endeavor for many communities. It must start and end with engagement; planning for the future means protecting water systems and resources for the next generations. Ultimately, each generation should leave the local water system in a better state than when they inherited it.

It was found that the price of water has a major influence on the amount of water consumed. Municipalities either charge a flat-rate for water, meaning houses are charged the same price for water no matter how much water is used (commonly in places without water meters) or they are charge based on volume. With household metering, users are more aware of how much water they are using and the cost associated with it. Though water is often priced quite low, volume-based water pricing has shown to drastically decrease household usage. In 2011, 58 percent of Canadian households had water meters. The installation of more meters resulted in a decrease in daily water use "by 27 percent from 342 liters per person in 1991 to 251 litres per person in 2011."[5]

The Okanagan basin is an example of a community whose major industries involve agriculture and tourism. Diagram 3 clearly shows that water demands for crops, lawn maintenance, and golf courses

5 "Residential Water Use in Canada," Environment Canada, accessed February 2015. https://www.ec.gc.ca/indicateurs-indicators/default.asp?lang=en&n=7E808512-1

vastly outweigh all residential water use. Each community will need to focus on the areas that will have the greatest impact. For this community, water conservation policies, planning, and incentives for agricultural and tourism sectors could result in big reductions.

This picture of water use in the Okanagan Valley is not unlike our global profile. Agriculture is the largest user of freshwater in the world, accounting for 70 percent.[6] In many countries, water is pumped out of waterways for agriculture faster than it can be replenished and much of the water is sprayed and lost through evaporation.

Diagram 3 is the global sum of all freshwater withdrawals. These results are biased strongly by the few countries which have very high water withdrawals. When ratios are averaged for each individual country the ratios are 59 percent (agriculture), 23 percent (municipal) and 18 percent (industrial).

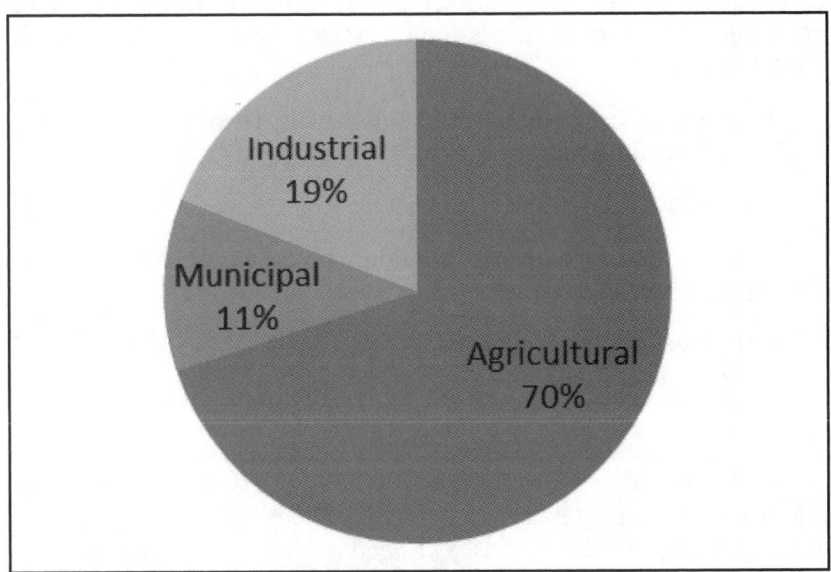

Diagram 3: Global Freshwater Use

Growing populations put greater pressures on freshwater systems for large-scale farm production. The food you eat has an invisible and embedded water footprint. For example, "the water footprint from beef cattle (15,400 m3/ton as a global average), is much larger than the footprints of meat from sheep (10,400 m3/ton), pig (6,000 m3/ton), goat (5,500 m3/ton), or chicken (4,300 m3/ton)."[7] Most of

6  "Water Uses," Aquastat, Food and Agriculture Organization of the United Nations, accessed March 2015. http://www.fao.org/nr/water/aquastat/water_use/index.stm
7  "Product Water Footprints: Animal Products," Water Footprint, accessed February 2015. http://www.waterfootprint.org/?page=files/Animal-products

this is embedded in the food the cow consumes. On the other end, a kilogram of vegetables takes 300 to 400 liters of water to produce. Clearly, eating "at the top of the food chain" has a big impact on environmental resources. As a system, we need to consider the type of food we eat and waste to relieve pressure on our water systems.

## 3. Reducing Water Pollution

Although bodies of water have the capacity to break down some substances, those capacities can be overcome by the quantities of waste put into the system. Organic material, such as sewage waste, requires microbes to digest and break it down. When effluent levels overreach the capacity of the microbes, the water can become polluted and overrun with waste.

Industries and manufacturing plants are among the largest contributors of polluting substances, which includes phosphates, lead, and other heavy metals such as mercury. Other major sources include the following:

- Commercial and household substances, such as cleaners, car washes, and soaps.

- Pesticides and fertilizers from lawns, golf courses, and agriculture.

- Water runoff from roads containing oils, antifreeze, and other petroleum substances.

- Sewage outflow and septic systems.

- Medical substances (passed through humans and discarded as waste).

Wetlands and marsh areas act as nature's filters, with bacteria and microbes that can digest an array of substances. Unfortunately, much of the wetlands of the world have been drained and developed into commercial and residential areas. In urban systems, mini-wetland areas can be established to help control pollutant levels before they enter other waterways. For example, rain gardens are depressions that catch water runoff that are placed adjacent to roads. The native plants in the rain garden help filter and store water so it can enter groundwater systems, rather than directly flowing into sewer pipes or streams. Rain gardens are also valuable for flood control, as they can capture and absorb water.

To control pollution, it is best to tackle it at the source, rather than treating it downstream. It is smart for communities to invest in source-control to avoid pollution issues in the future. This requires tracing pollutants back to the source. They may come from residents, industry, commercial, or government use. Restricting certain polluting products and promoting alternatives can help mitigate the use of harmful substances that will undoubtedly enter the waterway if they are sold in stores.

How to help reduce pollution at the source:

- Lobby for a ban of the use of toxic substances in commercial or industrial processing.

- Educate residences and businesses about cleaning and household products, how to reduce usage, and which ones to avoid.

- Avoid plant fertilizers with phosphorus (they can cause algal blooms).

- Look at specific sectors such as food services, dry cleaning, dental, and medical to identify and alleviate specific sources of water contaminants.

- Plant rain gardens to capture road runoff in your local community and in your neighborhood.

- Start a campaign to reduce top water pollutants in your community.

How to keep park waters clean:

- Have proper recycling and garbage receptacles available at parks to keep debris out of waterways.

- Conduct an annual park clean up and collect trash from the edges of water where waste tends to collect.

- Install composting toilet systems in parks with natural-filtering process.

## 4. Reducing Water Use in Our Homes

Discharged water from our sinks, showers, dishwashers, and laundry machines is called gray water, and the effluent from toilets is called black water. New home designs have started to incorporate gray-water systems, which capture water from sinks and showers for reuse in toilets. It is estimated that toilet flushing represents up to one-third of water use in homes. Reclaiming gray water for a second use can drastically reduce the water footprint of a home (see Diagram 4).

Coupled with low-flow faucets, showerheads, and toilets, homes can easily reduce water consumption in half. Gray water can also be mildly treated and used in lawn irrigation.

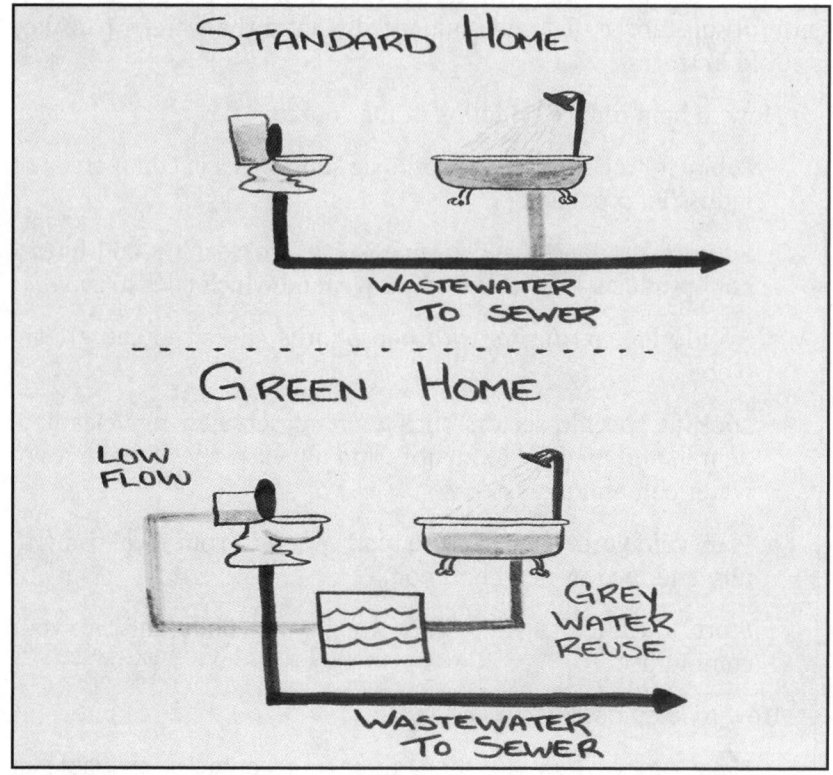

Diagram 4: Gray Water Use

Water is a global issue, but you can start to tackle it and do your part in your home and community. After all, that is where all the great water-protecting movements have stemmed from! What you can do as an individual:

- Fix leaky faucets and septic tanks to reduce wasted water and pollution.

- Install aerators on sinks, and low-flow showerheads and toilets.

- Reduce your irrigation time in half, only water during cooler hours of the day. In addition, install direct-drip irrigation to reduce evaporation rates.

- Let your grass grow above three inches in length. Longer grass reduces the need for watering and the roots reach deeper, which filters storm water as it passes through the soil. The grass will also stay green longer!

- Use a broom to clean decks and driveways, rather than a water hose.

- Recycle your used motor oil, paints, and antifreeze instead of dumping them.

- Replace asphalt driveways with pavers for better drainage into the soil.

- Install rain barrels to capture and reuse rainfall.

- Redirect gutters to flow into rain barrels or green space instead of hard surfaces that flow into storm drains.

- Wash cars on lawns, ideally without harmful car wash solutions.

- Plant native species and reduce lawn space to avoid using pesticides and excessive watering.

- Tell your local government officials that water conservation and quality is an important issue; make recommendations for community action.

# 8
# *Renewable Energy: Seeking the Net-Zero Community*

If you are reading this book, you are likely the type of person who gets excited when you see solar panels on a roof in your neighborhood. Solar panels, wind systems, and other sources of alternative energy represent more than kilowatts; they are symbols of self-sufficiency, resilience, and progress towards a better future. While the energy grid has given a great resource to society, there is room for more alternative energy that can be produced at both a small and community scale. These energy sources are driven by renewable resources and natural forces, such as wind, tidal waves, and solar energy.

Renewable energy is important because of the benefits it provides to the environment, to the local economy, and to energy security. Unlike fossil fuel resources, which are finite, renewable energy sources such as wind and solar are infinite supply.

There is also a strong community investment aspect to green energy. Most renewable energy investments are spent on materials and local workmanship to build and maintain technologies, rather than on costly energy imports. Renewable energy investments are usually spent within the United States, frequently in the same state, and often in the same town. This means your energy dollars stay local and help create jobs and increase local economic growth. A green economy is a diverse economy, and this provides a sense of energy security as we become less reliant on the fluctuating prices of fossil fuels.

Human activity has been overburdening our atmosphere with carbon emissions for more than 100 years so by going green there is little to no greenhouse gas emissions. Evidence of human induced climate change continues to mount and while we tend to bank on our countries policies or a new technology to make a turn around, the most significant and immediate change can be made at the community level.

## 1. Why We Care about Climate Change

Though scientists have been ringing the alarm bell about climate change for decades, it wasn't until the movie *An Inconvenient Truth* was released that the world's general population became aware of the causes and threats of climate change.

You've heard the numbers about global warming, let's focus on why we should be concerned. What will happen in our communities as the earth and oceans warm?

### 1.1 Sea-level rise

As half of the world's population lives near coasts, sea-level rise is a serious concern. Some of the biggest cities in the US are on the coasts, much of them in low lying areas. If your community is near the ocean, it's worth talking with others in your community about what these types of changes could mean.

### 1.2 Increased forest fires

The increase in heat waves means drier summer conditions creating the risk of forest fires. Threatening California wildfires have become more common over the last ten years. Communities near forests already consider fire response, but should be preparing for increased activity.

### 1.3 Natural environment impacts

Ecosystems will change and shift as local climate changes, forcing species to adapt by moving to new areas to avoid destruction. This means new critters could be coming to your neighborhood and some familiar ones leaving. This also holds true for trees and other vegetation and you may already notice some species under stress from the changing climate.

## 1.4 Food impacts

More carbon in the atmosphere means more carbon in the oceans. This is already changing the seas and putting many creatures at risk. It could also dramatically change the availability of fish stocks that we rely on for a food source.

The fluctuating temperatures also make it very challenging for farmers to grow food. They seek consistency to grow their crops each year. Both of these impacts could change the way our food systems function.

## 1.5 Water supply

Warmer conditions and sporadic rain have resulted in less snowpack in the mountains and less recharging of grand water aquifers. Areas where water is currently plentiful will have to be more cautious in the management of freshwater supplies.

You may feel like humans can adapt to these changes, but when you look at the above impacts more closely, you see a pattern. Adaptation will commonly mean greater costs to all goods and products we buy in the coming decades. Focusing on renewable energy sources now, will benefit us and the generations to come.

While *An Inconvenient Truth* painted a dark picture of the impacts of climate change, it spurred action around the globe. Local governments, city officials, and engaged citizens have become the champions for taking action on climate change.

# 2. Renewable Energy in Your Community

Renewable energy technologies such as solar and heat-exchange systems have continually evolved over the last 30 years and investment has greatly increased over the last 5 years. The commitment to energy and carbon reductions in some countries have made them world leaders in green energy development and provided testing grounds for the rest of the world. One of those leaders is the United States, which is the second largest producer of clean energy in the world (112 Billion kWh). However this represents only 2.7 percent of the overall electricity generation in the US, compared to the 10.7 percent in Germany which has the largest percentage of clean energy generation in the world.[1]

Clean energy has evolved to a point at which governments and businesses in North America can now make a strong case for integrating

---

1  "Delivering on Renewable Energy Around the World: How Do Key Countries Stack Up?" Jake Schmidt and Aaron Haifly, Natural Resources Defense Council (NRDC), accessed March 2015. http://www.nrdc.org/energy/files/delivering-renewable-energy.pdf

the technology, but how does this translate into action that you can take on a community and individual level? There are two options for you to consider, which are discussed further in the following sections:

- Install green energy technology in your home and encourage others to do the same. (These technologies are highlighted in sections 2.1 to 2.6.)

- Buy carbon offsets or green energy from an independent provider (see section 4.).

The viability and effectiveness of most technologies is greatly affected by geography. For example solar availability is limited by your latitude, orientation of your home, and the annual cloud cover, which all affect the total sunlight you receive. Other key factors include different maintenance requirements of the systems and a range of cost factors.

The following sections provide you with a background of the different types of green energy systems that are gradually developing. Of the following, the common trait is they can all function without the use of fossil fuels.

## 2.1 Photovoltaic solar panels

Photovoltaic (PV) solar panels generate electricity by the absorption of sunlight through silicone cells which is then transferred directly to the electrical grid or a bank of batteries. The benefits include:

- Low-operating and low-maintenance costs compared to costs of other renewable energy systems.

- There are no mechanical moving parts, meaning limited breakdowns.

- Photovoltaic panels make no noise.

- They are relatively easy to install.

The disadvantages are the reliance on sunlight and the seasonal and weather-related variations that come with it. There is also the concern that if the panel itself does get damaged, it cannot be repaired, and a full panel replacement is needed. The cost of solar panels has previously been a significant barrier; however, the price has significantly dropped due to increasing markets in the US, Ontario, and Europe and due to less expensive production in China. A noticeable drop has occurred over the last five years, making the payback much more desirable for most North Americans. According to Bloomberg New Energy

Finance, in 1971 the silicon PV cells in dollar-per-watt was $76.67; in 2014, it was $0.36.[2]

A great example is Germany's commitment to solar energy, which has been astounding. It has developed to a point where on some days 50 percent of Germany's energy demand is being met by solar PV plants installed throughout the country.[3] Keep in mind, if you are concerned about a lack of sun in your area, most of North America has the same or better levels of solar availability as Germany, so if it can work there, it can work here!

## 2.2 Solar hot water systems

Solar hot water systems (SHW) are often confused with solar PV panels because of their reliance on the sun. For SHW, the sun heats a liquid of some form (i.e., water or glycol), which is then transferred to the home water tank or to a radiant floor-heating system.

These systems can be very effective and there has been great uptake in Germany and Hawaii, both where energy costs are high. However, the effectiveness of the systems can vary greatly and there is a maintenance component to consider. The glycol in the heating system must be tested regularly as it breaks down over time, and so called "burned" glycol can permanently damage a system.

## 2.3 Geo-exchange systems

We're not all engineers, so let's keep this simple. You know how your fridge works? Heat is drawn from inside your refrigerator and dispersed from the coils at the back. This is the same technology that is used in geo-exchange heating. The unique part of this technology is that the process can be reversed back and forth to provide heating and cooling.

The general idea of this technology is to take advantage of the ground's heating and cooling properties to heat or cool buildings. The "exchange" between the ground and the building is achieved by using a pump and a form of compressor to move some form of liquid from the constant temperature of the ground to the surface.

The consistent temperature of the ground past five feet of depth offers the temperature difference to provide heating and cooling to a building. Getting the heat out of the ground can be expensive, as deep

2 "PV Market Status," EnergyTrend of TrendForce Corp., accessed March 2015. http://pv.energytrend.com/

3 "Performance of Photovoltaics (PV) in Germany," SMA Solar Technology AG, accessed February 2015. http://www.sma.de/en/company/pv-electricity-produced-in-germany.html

wells are drilled into the ground or coiled loops are installed horizontally over a wide area. The excavation required to install these wells and loops adds significant costs to this technology and is commonly recommended for new builds when site excavation is occurring.

You will also hear terms like "ground-source" and "geo-thermal" used when people are describing these systems, although geo-thermal is commonly considered a reference to ground steam found in places like Iceland.

These systems are a significant up-front investment with a long payback, but can be an attractive "free-energy" feature during resale. Look out for these types of systems in your community and find out more from the installers and from those who live in homes heated this way.

Learn more about geo-exchange systems online:

- United States: www.geoexchange.org

- Canada: www.geo-exchange.ca

## 2.4 Biomass or bioenergy

Another type of heating that is being considered for larger buildings is biomass. This involves the burning of organic materials to generate heat for a building. New biomass systems have improved the combustion system to a point where emissions and particulate are greatly minimized resulting in a much lower carbon footprint. These systems are for larger buildings generally, so for your home you will have to stick with your fireplace for burning organic material for now. However, commercial and industrial applications are being installed in some communities.

## 2.5 Wind power

Although the idea of wind-power generation is a great idea, it might not the best investment for your home. Wind-power generators need strong and consistent airstreams and most residential areas are not ideal for this because of trees, buildings, and other geographical features. However, if you live in a windy coastal or mountainous area, this option may work for you. If you want to look into it further, the US Department of Energy has a consumer guide available for Small Wind Electric Systems.[4]

---

4 "Small Wind Electric Systems: A US Consumer's Guide," US Department of Energy, accessed March 2015. http://apps2.eere.energy.gov/wind/windexchange/pdfs/small_wind/small_wind_guide.pdf

## 2.6  Hydro power

Hydro-electric power or hydropower is the continuous flow of water which creates energy that can be captured and converted into energy. The most common type of hydro-electric power plant uses a dam on a river to store water in a reservoir. Water released from the reservoir flows through a turbine, spinning it, which in turn activates a generator to produce electricity. However, hydro-electric power doesn't necessarily require a large dam. Some hydro-electric power plants use a small canal to channel the river water through a turbine.

Hydro-electric power is often regarded as a green alternative to coal and other fossil fuel sources used to generate electricity. However, there are other hidden impacts that are not included in the carbon footprint of hydro energy. While hydropower does not generate air quality impacts, the construction and operation of dams significantly affect natural river flows and impact fish, wildlife, and livelihoods. The recently completed Three Gorges Dam on the Yangtze River in China submerged 13 cities, 140 towns, and 1,300 villages forcing 1.5 million people to relocate.[5]

## 3.  Do-It-Yourself Solar Collector

Are there some simpler options for your home? The best one that we have found is the Do-It-Yourself solar collector.

There are some great examples of homemade solar collectors that could provide some extra warmth when you need it. Check online and you will find some very creative solutions. The simplest, and most fun, involves collecting a bunch of aluminum cans and integrating them into a wooden panel. By putting holes in the cans and painting them black, air that enters the bottom of the panel will be heated as it passes through the cans, which can then be funneled into your home, shed, or greenhouse — a fun project that is worth trying. In the colder months, this little bit of additional heat can help to reduce your energy bills.

Here's a great video on how one man has built his own solar collector: http://faircompanies.com/videos/view/heating-seattle-back-yard-shed-with-soda-cans-as-solar-panels/. Try it for yourself first and then share your experience with your neighbors and help them build their own!

---

5 "Great Wall Across the Yangtze," PBS, accessed March 2015. http://www.pbs.org/itvs/greatwall/dam1.html

# 4. Carbon Offsets

There is another way to incorporate green energy so that you reduce your carbon footprint in a different way. If a project takes place that makes a significant carbon reduction (e.g., a windmill project), they can sell the "carbon credit" to a marketplace for the amount of emissions it has reduced. In the example of wind power, if it is replacing the need for coal-generated power, then there is a direct reduction in emissions. These projects can only become verifiable offsets if they would not have taken place without the investment from a carbon marketplace. That means, when a carbon credit is purchased, it is truly an investment in a green project that reduces the risk of climate change. This works great for projects like renewable energy, because often dirty energy is cheap, so it is hard to get renewable energy off the ground without the investment from a carbon-offset fund. Now, if a business or individual would like to calculate their emission sources and offset them to become carbon neutral, they can invest in a carbon fund and purchase enough credits to cover their impact.

For example, a burger joint in Victoria decided it wanted to become carbon neutral. The business measured its impact and it came to approximately 60 tonnes of carbon. The business purchased offsets for 60 tonnes of carbon ($30/tonne, $1,800 total) to become carbon neutral.

Some communities have started their own carbon fund in order to generate a pool of investment for green projects in their community. Typically, a nonprofit or local municipality manages the fund, and uses it to invest locally in new green projects such as solar panels on schools, heat pumps, boiler upgrades, switching fuel type to biodiesel, and more.

From here, the average resident or business can buy the credit to offset the carbon emissions they have generated. Buying enough credits to cover your carbon footprint for the year, you have offset your emissions and can declare that you are "carbon neutral."

Concerns around carbon offsets stem from high-profile projects that have generated credibility issues, but carbon offsets can be a fantastic tool to move towards a greener community. It creates the ability to invest in new green infrastructure that would otherwise have a poor return on investment (ROI) financially. Offset projects can measurably reduce carbon impacts in local communities, and are a part of the toolkit of solutions to fight climate change both at a local and global level. If you are considering purchasing offsets, or starting a fund, it is important to consider the following:

- The location of the offset project.

- The social benefits of the project as well as the environmental.

- The longevity of the project such as whether or not it will have a permanent impact.

- Verification such as the project is verified by a credible third party.

You can review different types of offset providers using online directories such as: The Carbon Catalog (www.carboncatalog.org/providers).The David Suzuki Foundation also provides a great resource on selecting carbon offsets in Canada and it endorses certified offsets from several providers including the well-respected Gold Standard (www.goldstandard.org). It is generally considered to be the highest standard for carbon offsets in the world and only focuses on offsets from energy efficiency and renewable energy projects. It also excludes tree planting projects, which are now seen as a less desirable method of reducing carbon because of variability of tree growth in different climates, annual fluctuations, and the length of time to make real reductions.[6]

---

### Carbon Tax: BC Shows the Possibilities

In 2008, the Province of British Columbia instituted a carbon tax to support the emission-education targets that were set at the same time. This carbon tax added an additional cost to carbon-based fuels. The tax started at the lower amount of $10 per tonne of green-house gasses and then gradually increased each year to $30 per tonne (7.2 cents CAN at the pumps). The funds from the tax are returned directly to general revenues. Five years later, the results show that overall emissions in the province have been reduced.

The intent of the carbon tax is to discourage fossil fuel consumption and reward those who produce less. There are concerns with carbon tax such as its fairness and that it is too difficult to really put a price on carbon emissions. If the dollar really is the bottom line, then the carbon tax has shown to be an option that fairly provides an incentive to drivers and home owners to consider using lower carbon fuels.

---

6 "Purchasing Carbon Offsets: A Guide for Canadian Consumers, Businesses, and Organizations," David Suzuki Foundation and Pembina Institute, accessed March 2015. http://www.davidsuzuki.org/publications/downloads/2009/climate_offset_guide.pdf

## 5. Purchasing Renewable Energy

Did you know that you can buy green energy? This is a variation of the purchasing of carbon offsets, but has a simple, more direct approach. This is how it works. An energy company produces green energy from one of the above listed technologies (see sections 2.1 to 2.6) and either puts this energy into the main grid or stores the energy. When you make a purchase of this green energy from the supplier, you can then consume energy knowing that you have contributed to green energy within the grid. This is an indirect method, but it's perfectly valid.

The US Environmental Protection Agency (EPA) provides a long list of green energy sources via their Green Power Locator (epa.gov/greenpower/pubs/gplocator.htm), but options are increasing gradually in Canada too. For example, Bullfrog Power (www.bullfrogpower.com) is a green energy provider that offers clean energy to home owners and businesses.

Depending on where you live in North America, you pay between $0.08 and $0.30 per kWh for energy.[7] If you spread the additional cost of renewable energy into cost per kWh over the life span of the technology, your will realize how affordable it could be. To cover this additional cost, you should also look to reduce consumption at the same time. Our energy has been historically inexpensive on a global scale and conservation is the easiest way to save a kWh. Find other ways to reduce your consumption by 20 percent at home and you can invest those savings in green energy! Think about the long-term cost to you and the environment and you will find that renewable energy makes sense for your community.

---

7  "Comparison of Electricity Prices in Major North American Cities," Hydro Quebec, accessed March 2015. http://issuu.com/hydroquebec/docs/comp_2014en?e=1151578/4165830

# 9
# *Recycling, Composting, and Trash*

This chapter focuses on dealing with the different types of waste that our society produces. Despite our experience, managing the waste we generate in our homes in an environmentally responsible way still provides challenges.

As our lives have improved over the last 80 years, we have greatly increased the amount of materials we consume. A study by the World Bank showed that the richest 20 percent of the world's population consumes 77 percent of the goods.[1] This disparity in consumption also produces an imbalance in the waste that is produced. However, there are many things that you can take control of to reduce the waste that is generated in your community.

The United States Environmental Protection Agency (EPA) reported that "in 2012, Americans generated 251 million tons of trash," almost a ton of waste per person.[2] This amount of garbage would fill

---

1 *2008 World Bank Development Indicators,* The International Bank for Reconstruction and Development/The World Bank, accessed March 2015. http://data.worldbank.org/sites/default/files/wdi08.pdf

2 "Municipal Solid Waste Generation, Recycling, and Disposal in the United States: Facts and Figures for 2012," United States Environmental Protection Agency (EPA), accessed February 2015. http://epa.gov/epawaste/nonhaz/municipal/pubs/2012_msw_fs.pdf

the Grand Canyon every two years! The good news is that after 40 years of continually increasing disposal fees, waste generation finally started to level out ten years ago. About one-third of waste generated is now recycled in some way, which is something we can greatly improve on!

Recycling began in the 1980s with the basics (e.g., paper, metal, and plastic) as markets emerged for their use. Recycling rates did not surpass 15 percent until 1990, but then grew significantly over the next 15 years. Since 2005, recycling participation has grown, but much more slowly as we take on the challenge of more complex waste including organic materials.

If you picked up this book, you are already miles beyond these fundamentals. What we are going to do is provide some new ways of dealing with common wastes and show you some remarkably innovative ideas that you can do at home or work, or that you can encourage your community members to consider.

## 1. Reduce, Reuse, Recycle

There are three main concerns for us when it comes to garbage disposal:

- Our waste inflicts multiple impacts to our land, water, and air.

- Managing the waste we create costs a lot of money, usually through taxes.

- Waste-management facilities take up large areas of land.

Think about where your garbage goes in your community. Landfills have greatly evolved over the last 40 years but they still generate nasty leachates and airborne emissions as their contents decompose. The modern landfill is built with leachate and air emission collection systems below, alongside, and within to catch the toxic runoff and gases that are generated by our trash. More modern landfill operations are also capturing the methane that is generated and turning it into energy. The methane produced in a landfill is a significant source of greenhouse gas emissions, but if we reduce the organic material in the landfill through composting, methane emissions are almost eliminated.

In Germany, they do something that terrifies many people in North America. They burn their garbage in an incinerator and turn it into energy. They find the North American's way of throwing trash onto a big pile and covering it with dirt just as crude! However, the Germans are not throwing everything into the burner and they follow the same mantra you have heard many times before: Reduce, Reuse, and Recycle!

Here are some ideas on how to *reduce* waste:

- Make less waste in the first place through the purchasing decisions you make.

- Find products that don't use a lot of packaging.

- Ask for junk mail to not be delivered to your home.

- Buy nontoxic products whenever possible.

- Think before you discard items!

The following includes ideas of how to *reuse* materials:

- Use reusable shopping bags instead of plastic bags.

- Use lunch containers and bags that are reusable.

- Find ways to reuse containers, boxes, and coffee cans.

- Make the most of your paper by using both sides (e.g., a child's art projects).

- Use cutlery and dishes that can be washed, not disposable.

- Store leftovers in reusable containers.

- Make old clothes into other textile items such as cushion covers or teapot cozies.

Of course, *recycle* everything:

- Divert as much waste from the landfill as possible.

- Buy products that can be recycled and that are made from recycled materials.

- Avoid buying hazardous material, which cannot be recycled.

These three goals still apply today, but they have evolved into some more comprehensive systems of materials management. So let's look to move beyond the basics for the individual, let's talk about how we can broaden our horizons and start tackling the more challenging two-thirds of our waste generation.

Take a look at how long the following things take to decompose:

- Paper: 6 weeks.

- Kitchen scraps: 1 to 6 months.

- Plastics: 20 to 1,000 years (depending on the thickness).

- Styrofoam: *Never* decomposes.

A key driver to creating a market for recycling is government policy. Policy can be put into place by the government, which suddenly sparks a marketplace. If you see waste that needs to be better managed in your community, engage your local government office and ask if there are ways things can be improved. Find examples from around the world that could be used in your community.

Here's a great example: The City of San Francisco recently placed a ban on plastic checkout bags which includes all retail stores and food establishments. If a shopper doesn't bring his or her own bag, the person will be charged ten cents per bag. The purpose of the Checkout Bag Ordinance is to reduce the impact of disposable bags on the city and the environment. A ten cent charge per checkout bag can reduce the amount of disposable bags used by nearly 70 to 90 percent![3] Something your community might be interested in, too?

## 1.1 Composting

Kitchen scraps and other organic material not only can take up one-third of landfill space, but they are also the primary generator of waste-related greenhouse gases. Managing your kitchen scraps with a composter at home (along with basic material recycling) is the best way to reduce the waste that your home sends to the landfill.

There are many excellent designs for backyard-composting units that will provide rich, nutrient-filled material for your garden on a regular basis. However, cooked food and meat products cannot be composted in regular backyard units. Some municipalities are starting to provide curbside kitchen-scrap collection for residents, but if this is not available, and you are really serious about processing all organics at home, there are more advanced home-composting units that will process all organic materials within a few days. These units will use extra energy and come at an additional cost, but it might be right for you.

The real epidemic for North Americans is that we waste so much food that could have been eaten. The US Department of Agriculture (USDA) found that 31 percent of the food produced goes uneaten,[4] so

3 "Checkout Bag Ordinance," SF Environment, accessed February 15. http://sfenvironment.org/article/prevent-waste/checkout-bag-ordinance
4 "The Estimated Amount, Value, and Calories of Postharvest Food Losses at the Retail and Consumer Levels in the United States," Jean C. Buzby, Hodan F. Wells, and Jeffrey Hyman, A Report Summary from the Economic Research Service, United States Department of Agriculture, accessed February 2015. http://endhunger.org/PDFs/2014/USDA-Food-Loss-2014-Summary.pdf

try to make the most of the food you purchase and you will save 30 percent on your food costs.

To take action on the community level, find out first if and how organics collection is provided in your community. Is it provided by the local government or by private contractors? Where does the organic material eventually end up? If you don't have organic processing in your community, work with your local waste authority, or with your local community association to get one started. If that doesn't work, create your own!

---

**Fun Section: Compost Bin Origami**

Go online to watch a great video about six-year-old Bella from Ottawa, Ontario, making an origami newspaper compost bin liner (https://www.youtube.com/watch?v=BfEX85V9n8w).

---

## 1.2  Plastics

We generate more plastics than ever, which are generated from petroleum products. All of these plastics can be recovered and reused in different ways, but it's not an easy material to process. Plastics come in many different forms, identified by the numbering system you find under each item, and that makes for extra complications in the separation process. Plastics also include dyes and other additives that need to be managed in a separate process. All of this requires more energy and creates more emissions and waste.

The solution? Avoid plastic or minimize the use of existing plastics as much as possible.

## 1.3  Batteries

Disposable batteries are still used extensively for a range of products, and their disposal into regular garbage bins has several environmental concerns. Batteries are made from an assortment of chemicals, including nickel and cadmium, which are extremely toxic to humans and the environment. For example, cadmium can cause damage to soil micro-organisms but can also bio-accumulate in fish. They also take 100 years to decompose in a landfill.

Avoiding disposable battery use is the ideal option. Fortunately, smartphones, tablets, and laptops use lithium ion batteries, which overall generates less waste materials. When you make other electronic purchases, try to avoid batteries in the first place, but if you must, look for rechargeable battery options. Rechargeable batteries last half as long as a regular disposable battery per charge, but you can recharge on average about 100 times. This means each rechargeable battery results in 49 fewer regular batteries needed. Rechargeable batteries can cost four to five times more, but by recharging you will save 80 percent over their life span when compared to regular batteries.

To properly dispose of both regular and rechargeable batteries, there is a fantastically simple service in North America called Call-2Recycle. It is North America's first and largest battery stewardship program. Since 1996, this group has diverted more than 85 million pounds (39 million kilograms) of batteries and cellphones from the solid-waste stream in the US and Canada. Call2Recycle is a nonprofit that collects, ships, and recycles batteries at zero cost. They provide the boxes and once filled, seal and send! You will be amazed how quickly people will help fill the box with the batteries that were hiding in their homes.

This is a great opportunity for you to lead change throughout the community. Ask other key businesses and facilities in your community to consider providing this service. For example, a recreation center is a great spot at which regular visitors can drop off old batteries.

## 1.4 Styrofoam

If there is one product that you need to avoid in your purchasing, it's Styrofoam. While it does not emit chemicals to the environment as much as one would think, the primary concern is that it is impossible to break down naturally.

Some places it is hard to avoid, as Styrofoam is still used in many restaurants for take-out and leftover foods. Encourage your local restaurants to make the switch from Styrofoam to a more organic material. Or bring your own container for leftovers. To get restaurants to act, get them to understand the promotional benefits of switching away from Styrofoam which will help cover any additional costs related to the switch. Ensure they understand that the younger generation is looking for this switch when they go to restaurants.

Styrofoam is reused for many applications these days, but there is usually a cost to dispose. We need to change the way items are packaged and eliminate items that do not breakdown. Ask the store you purchased the product from to take back the Styrofoam, but make sure they don't just throw it in the garbage.

## 1.5 Mattresses

Matresses are a good example of a moxed material product (e.g., made of metal, fabric, and plastic) that can be difficult to separate into a usable material again. In September 2013, California enacted the *Used Mattress Recovery and Recycling Act*,[5] which requires mattress manufacturers to create a statewide recycling program for discarded mattresses. The state now requires retailers to take responsibility for discarding their customers' old mattresses. Retailers must now receive old mattresses at no cost to a resident when delivering a new mattress at a customer's home.

Why are we focusing on mattresses here? To make a point that most everything you own can be recycled now and those systems are only getting better. The limiting factors include the time it takes to recycle a unique item, and not everything can be recycled for free. Most items have a repurpose option, but it is up to all of us to take the extra time to ask questions about disposal before we buy the items. The business has the expertise to manage the waste associated with its product, so hold the business accountable.

# 2. Set a Lofty Goal: Zero-Waste Work, School, and Home

Want to make an impact in your community? Set the bar high and inspire others to make changes. Help set a goal of zero waste at work, school, and home and change the way waste is managed at your work or, if you're a student, at your school. You will find coworkers and students who want to help champion this goal and then others will take the message back to their homes. In some communities, you will find the schools have better recycling systems than many workplaces.

Working with a few key people can help to make long-lasting change in your community, so start by changing actions where people spend most of their day. People are also more likely to respond as an organization, where others will keep everyone accountable, as compared to home where we all tend to be a little lazier in our commitments!

Encourage others in your community to set goals for waste reduction. You may find an opportunity to help support the recycling of a specific waste that your community has not addressed yet. One worth looking into is plastic bags which are legendary for their rapid accumulation in our landfills and oceans.

---

5 Senate Bill No. 254, California Legislative Information, accessed February 2015.
   http://leginfo.legislature.ca.gov/faces/billNavClient.xhtml?bill_id=201320140SB254

## 3. Consumer-to-Consumer Selling and the Sharing Economy

The dramatic increase of community-based reselling of goods over the last five years has greatly extended the life span of good and products that would have either been disposed of, or unnecessarily recycled. By reusing a local product, you avoid production of one less product that needs to be shipped from overseas or across land by producers.

It started with eBay, an online auction site which exploded on the scene in 1995 during the "dot-com" era. This made way for simple peer-to-peer selling online, which moved the old "for sale" ads in the newspaper to online. Sites such as Kijiji, launched by eBay, have made the old-school Sunday garage sale into an everyday obsession with finding a great deal. Many of you are already using this service, but just a reminder; this is a huge environmental success as well.

In the small town of Grand Forks, British Columbia, a Facebook page was started by a community member for swapping and posting goods. The page is very active and popular, serving the needs of the specific community. Online hubs, such as these, can be a great way to extend the life of goods and keep them out of landfills.

People, who like to fix things, can resell old goods in good-as-new shape. There are other ways to keep it local as well including clothing swaps and community or block garage sales. The sharing economy is starting to change the way we use items and helping to eliminate major purchases and unnecessary consumerism. The following examples show some repurchases that make the biggest environmental impact and what can be done:

- Computers contain a range of mysterious metals and mixed materials. Rather than scrapping your old electronics, they can be rebuilt, or used for parts. They could also be donated to charities who can fix them and then distribute these simple computing systems to those in need.

- Share your home when you are not using it (see Airbnb.ca).

- Share or rent your stuff with others using a range of other sites. Some examples include:

  - TaskRabbit.com: A marketplace to hire for jobs and tasks.

  - Spinlister.com: A site where you can rent your bike, surfboard, or skis.

- Vinted.com: Described as an online consignment store.

To get a full picture of how our purchasing decisions impact the generation of waste, the Story of Stuff (http://storyofstuff.org/) provides an excellent description of the process and impacts of our consumption patterns.

## 4. Upcycling

Upcycling is a way to recycle. It is the process of gaining a new use from something that can no longer be used for its original purpose. This maximizes the benefit a material can provide and creates one less waste overall.

A good example of a business that embraced this philosophy is Interface Inc., a carpeting company that has become a legend in the sustainable business world. The company started integrating recovered fiber materials into its products in the early 1990s and launched a carpet-recovery program to secure more fibers. This eventually led to producing products with 100 percent recovered materials. Interface was also the first company to introduce a carbon offset via its Cool Carpet program. This early leadership and innovation turned company founder Ray C. Anderson into a pioneer of sustainable manufacturing.

Here are some other examples of upcycling:

- An old ladder becomes a bookshelf.

- A vintage suitcase becomes a chair.

- Old glass bottles become decorative lamps.

For more inspiration, check out UpcycleThat.com.

## 5. Circular Economy

What should we be aiming for? The ideal scenario is that we all work towards something called the "circular economy." The argument is that we need to move away from the linear "take, make, dispose" model which relies on large amounts of accessible resources and energy. The goal is to maximize efficiency by greatly reducing the use of resources and fossil fuels, and maximizing the reuse of materials.

In this system, companies have control over the products they produce and the energy and materials needed. This allows the company to have control over maintenance, reconditioning, and materials recovery. Customers only pay for the service needed and used. This creates a situation where the manufacturer has a greater incentive to make its product last. For example, Philips Lighting is exploring beyond just selling lighting products, and looking at collecting and recycling lamps as well.

The Ellen MacArthur Foundation website provides a detailed background on the topic of the circular economy and several leading examples (www.ellenmacarthurfoundation.org).

# 10
# *Natural Environment and Green Spaces*

Urban dwelling has become increasingly disconnected from nature. Even now, it can be hard to fathom how nature and a city can coexist in the same space. For the first time, the majority of human beings are classified as "urban." This will only continue to grow, as more people congregate to live in large cities.

Development over the past six decades, after World War II, has increased at an incredible pace. Families flocked to the outskirts of town to settle in what became the modern-day suburb. To meet demand, spec homes were constructed (designed to specifications, rather than custom built). The repercussions in some of these developments are a lack of consideration for the environment. Fifty years ago, it was unfathomable to build a multistory house with two washrooms and five bedrooms in eight weeks.

Fast-paced development has led to the modern city at odds with nature. Thus, on a national level, we have disconnected our communities and our lives from the ecosystems we depend on for survival.

This is reflected in our daily lives as we face conflicting decisions between man and nature: The city versus the outdoors; and working versus relaxing.

Research has shown that isolation from nature in urban environments can have negative impacts on our physical and mental health and also creates ignorance towards nature and how we need its functions to survive. The widely accepted biophilia hypothesis states that humans have an innate tendency to affiliate with other living organisms. In order to develop emotional, cognitive, and social potential, humans require contact with a diverse world.

In addition, natural environments provide critical life-enabling functions such as cleaning the air, detoxifying water, restricting erosion, providing habitat for other species, and decomposing waste. To re-create the fish in the river, oxygen in the air, and clean freshwater would be devastatingly costly to mankind. Thus, we must find ways to work with nature, rather than against it. This brings up two very important considerations: Integrating natural systems into our modern communities, and preserving natural areas. We will discuss both in this chapter.

## 1. Integrating Nature into Our Communities

Our communities need roads, buildings, power lines, and bridges — this entire infrastructure is a part of how we live — but we also need green space and natural systems. Lakes, rivers, forests, wetlands, grasslands, and even deserts exert ecological functions that are critical to our survival. Without plants, our air would be deprived of oxygen. Without healthy waterways, we would not have access to clean drinking water. Natural areas support abundant wildlife such as birds, insects, frogs, fish, and mammals. How do we balance our needs to develop with nature's needs, which are truly our needs as well? As global population grows, it is important to preserve and restore natural spaces and also look at how we can integrate ecology into our communities.

In one major US city I visited, I found there was only one species — humans. The area was void of anything else — no birds, no insects, not even an ant, butterfly, or bee flew in the air. This was a disturbing observation. At that moment, I turned to notice a man on his hands and knees, scrapping off a tiny patch of moss that was in a rock crevice. Is this the pinnacle of human success — to eradicate every other species? Or will we embrace other species, and plan our cities and communities to support a diverse ecology? I believe we should be working towards the latter option. We can take lessons from biodynamic farming, to show that many species can coexist in the same area if it is designed and maintained appropriately. So what would this look like on a practical level?

Our green spaces are a great place to start. The kind of landscape we are familiar with in our cities is often ornamental and serves little or no ecological purpose. These plants are frequently imported and require copious maintenance to survive — pruning, heavy watering, and fertilizing. Rather, these green spaces could be full of life, with native plant species that have innate relationships with other native species such as insects, birds, and small mammals. These green zones, even if they are in place for decorative functions, could be seen as opportunities to create small ecosystems. Shifting our cities from the gray concrete world we are familiar with to green, living cities will take determined planning and cooperation from many parties — but it is possible.

From an urban-planning perspective, most communities continue to treat ecological zones as separated from other land uses. Some progressive communities are breaking this divide and integrating ecology into cities, finding synergistic ways for both to exist. Two converging realizations — the dire state of our natural environment and the opportunity for communities to find green solutions — are inspiring architects, city planners, local citizens, and developers to find synergies between human infrastructure and nature's infrastructure. This is due to the realization that urban encroachment has put tremendous pressures on natural areas, so we need to look at cities as a system of a whole. We are now seeing local governments embrace sustainable transportation, energy-efficient buildings, living roofs, native plant gardens, and enhanced green space.

In some cities, bees have been placed on the roofs of buildings, and fruit trees planted in a nearby park. The fruit trees provide shade and food for the community in the fall. The bees produce honey and enhance pollination. We are far from seeing full ecological integration in a city, but some exciting new concepts are emerging to rethink urban design, community planning, and developmental process. You probably haven't considered a family outing to a local parking lot, or a nice hike in the suburbs? Developments all over the world are invigorating these conventional "dead zones" with green ways, trails, community garden spaces, and natural habitats. This experience of connecting with nature is something great cities offer.

In New York, the famous High Line (www.thehighline.org) offers an oasis — a piece of paradise — in the heart of one of the largest cities in the United States. The High Line is a public park, built on a historic elevated rail line above the streets of Manhattan. A controversial development at first, the High Line is now a tourist attraction and a favorite local spot. It hosts weddings, fashion shows, art installations, and numerous other events. Arguably, the High Line has enhanced both the city and the ecology. It took leadership from within the City of New York and community support to raise the funds to create and maintain this unique urban park. What first seemed impossible has now become a global inspiration for other communities.

The following can play a role in making something like this happen in your community:

- Landscape architects.

- Building architects and designers.

- Community planners.

- Property owners and developers.

- Nonprofit organizations working on conservation or land trusts.

- Local government staff.

- An individual or a group of engaged citizens who are willing to gather and lead a conversation with the above stakeholder groups.

All of these people can play a pivotal role in starting the conversation, leading an initiative, or shifting current developments to integrate ecology and green space.

These are some of the benefits of natural areas in cities:

- Create outdoor recreation opportunities.

- Attract ecotourism businesses and visitors.

- Beautification; health and wellness.

- Increase value of neighboring properties.

- Increase air quality and other ecosystem services.

- Provide environmental educational opportunities for local schools.

## 2. Preserving Natural Areas

While we need to integrate nature into our cities, it is also important to protect areas that remain relatively untouched and unaltered by development. These areas often support complete ecosystems and habitat for many species. In researching how these regional, state or provincial, and national parks are created, we noticed that it is often the outcome of ad hoc efforts by local groups and/or concerned citizens. Interestingly, in more cases than we expected, it was the people who came forward presenting the case for preservation to the government.

Communities can identify key natural areas within or surrounding the city and protect them from development. These areas are valuable not just for other species and ecosystem services that humans depend on, but they can create new economic opportunism. They can spawn tourism and health and wellness businesses as they often provide recreational opportunities.

Within the city, biologists can work with city planners to determine key areas that need special attention. This may include watersheds, migratory patterns and timing, nesting sites of rare and endangered species, invasive species threats, and keystone species. Most community-planning processes outline the basics of environmental aspects, but there is far more that can be done to integrate ecology and human landscapes. We can ask ourselves: What ecosystem elements pass through the city? Perhaps it is a river, migratory route for birds, or nesting site for turtles. How can your local community help to conserve and also enhance these areas?

My favorite park in Victoria is Gowlland Tod Provincial Park. The rain forest groves meet the ocean along a beautiful stretch of the West Coast. The park is rich in biodiversity, hosting more than 150 species, including some that are endangered such as the phantom orchid and Peale's peregrine falcon. In 1,200 hectares one can find tide pools, grassy meadows, mossy ravines, creeks, and tall trees. The marine life attracts scuba divers who can see well through the clear waters. Garry Oak meadows — one of the most at-risk ecosystems in Canada — is located throughout the park.

As one of the last remaining natural areas of Greater Victoria, I never assumed the possibility of not having Gowlland. It is an anchor of our community and is visited by hundreds of thousands of residents from nearby communities. It would be like New York without Central Park — unfathomable. What I came to learn is Gowlland was never initially intended by local government to be a park.

I met Eric Bonham in 2013. Now retired from his government job, yet still working on environmental causes, Bonham was an active member of a group who was the leading force behind the protection of this area. Over a pint at his favorite Scottish pub, he shared his story.

It was to be a large-scale and profitable development. At the time, hardly anyone thought to question this. With the land owned by a development firm, the writing was on the wall. This patch of nature would be uprooted, and the coastline changed to accommodate large, high-end homes, grassy lawns, fake beaches, and paved driveways. However, there were a few people that questioned if this fate was appropriate for a pristine patch of ecological diversity. Against all odds, a group of concerned citizens formed to discuss what could be done. They could not accept the dire fate of this land. It was too precious, too beautiful, and far too important.

The Gowlland Foundation was born and comprised of people from various backgrounds. Each member brought their experience, talent, and perspective to the table, and together, they met on weekends to discuss the plan to preserve the land.

"It was definitely and imminently going to be developed," Bonham explained. "The landowner was committed to developing the land and here was this fledgling group saying, 'Hey, wait a second' ... People really thought we were nuts, nevertheless we had a determined vision."

Starting in 1989, the Gowlland Foundation was as grassroots as it gets. The group was about 12 strong. The format was loose, but this unstructured group had something that kept them rooted: They shared an unwavering vision to protect the Gowlland Range through the creation of a park. How they would get there they weren't sure, but the end goal was crystal clear. The vision was the glue that kept the group moving forward. They rallied support, raised funds, lobbied government, wrote proposals, were denied, and tried again. People came and went, but the core group remained intact throughout the years. They took people on tours of the area (though they were technically trespassing on private land), ran campaigns to educate the public, and formed partnerships with other nonprofits to share the vision. Passion pushed them forward, and they faced all odds head on. They got charity status, which allowed them to raise money for the cause. They hosted concerts and engaged the arts community to raise awareness.

The Foundation struck an important balance between vision and pragmatism. The vision guided them, and their ideas translated directly to action. Participants had responsibility to complete tasks and propel the vision forward. They would talk amongst themselves, form a game plan, and get down to business. The Foundation worked tirelessly for several years, raising awareness and gaining the ear of the local politicians who could provide essential support.

The pivotal moment came when they formed a partnership with the Nature Conservancy of Canada. John Eisenhower, a senior representative from the Conservancy was intrigued and when the Foundation members took him on a tour of the area to be developed. He took one look at the vista and said, "We have to protect this."

This partnership was critical as the engagement of Nature Conservancy Canada in turn attracted the involvement of the Provincial Government and the interest of the Capital Regional District. The Foundation had done its work on the ground level, but to get complete commitment from government to turn this area into a permanent park required a greater force. As Bonham puts it, "It was time to bring in the big guys, in particular, the Provincial Government and the landowner." They worked together with Nature Conservancy Canada, and in 1995, the window of opportunity opened further with the timely announcement of the Commonwealth Heritage Legacy Program which was initiated by the province to preserve 14 percent of land throughout British Columbia with park protection status. The Gowlland Foundation used this lever to preserve the area resulting in the creation of the GowllandTod Provincial Park, which was officially opened on March 30th, 1994.

Years of work, many meetings, and countless emails later, the Gowlland Tod Provincial Park now exists and is protected in perpetuity. It contains 16 miles (25 kilometers) of nature trails and is home to deer, cougars, diving birds, hawks, tree frogs, bald eagles, river otters, and bears. Gowlland is a powerful story of what a small group of concerned citizens, with a common vision, can accomplish.

While the approach taken by the Gowlland Foundation may seem unorthodox, there are common threads that can be identified within community groups where efforts to preserve hav succeeded. In the case of Gowlland Tod Park initiative, you will find the following consistent themes:

• Strong vision understood by all members.

- The end goal was clear, but the means to get there remained flexible.

- Formed partnerships and leveraged resources.

- Connections to and allies within the government.

- Continual efforts to raise awareness.

- Connect the community back to nature.

Finding a patch of natural habitat without human interference is rare, and these areas act as safe homes for many species at risk and important ecosystems. Less and less of these areas remain. What is left should be considered for protection. Those that connect with the land will fight to preserve it.

# 11
# *Arts and the Environmental Movement*

The arts and sustainability are often put into different categories in official community plans and classroom education, but art plays a crucial role in how we express and interact with the natural world.

Art, and the process of making art, unlocks our creative capacity and helps us think differently. It tears conventional silos apart and exposes emotions and appreciation. Without really knowing it, the effects of art may be a reason for your affinity for nature. Paintings, music, and creative writing can enhance our relationship with nature and help us see it from different perspectives. Art is a wonderful education tool and a way to engage citizens of all ages.

Creative works enhance our city. A barren and decrepit wall can become a beautiful mural of sea life; an empty city square becomes alive with music and dancing. The creation of art can be a solo endeavor, exploring new ideas and concepts; or it can be a social gathering. Festivals, shows, and galleries are all places people congregate.

Visiting cities across the US, Canada, and Europe, it seemed like the most connected cities, the ones with a strong community and cultural ties, also had a strong arts presence (e.g., Austin, Portland, Berlin, Montreal). It seemed as though their culture was rooted in the arts, but this connectivity stemmed into other areas. Interestingly, these cities are also leaders in environmental action. It could be that the strong roots in the arts also bring forth a sense of connection with the natural world.

Robert Bateman's famous collection of paintings shows us the beauty and profoundness of nature's simple statements. Bateman has an incredible ability to bring a bird on a wire, a buffalo's breath, and the texture of an elephant into a perspective from which we can gain a stronger appreciation for other species. It's not just a picture. You look into the image and feel like you are sharing a moment with these beings, it's like you are right there.

Spoken word, poetry, and music often convey important environmental and social messages. Joni Mitchell famously sang, "They paved paradise and put up a parking lot," which got people thinking about their own towns and how they were developing. For generations environmental activists have used their thoughtful prose to bring awareness to their audience and fans. Some of the most successful environmental movements involved influential artists such as Neil Young and Pete Seeger.

Graphic facilitation, design, and motion-graphic art have taken complex sustainability topics and helped us understand the depth of topics such as climate change, acid rain, and the global food system. Infographics have brought a strong visual presence, summarizing massive reports into something you can read and understand in ten minutes. This art form is sharing information at a rapid pace, making it accessible to a broader population, who may not dig deep into scientific journals to get the facts.

Photography and videography have been powerful mediums for connecting global populations with some of the most remote places on earth. Seeing to the depths of the ocean and to the top of polar landscapes, this imagery has brought an awareness of endangered species and natural wonders that we may not ever see personally in our lifetime, but our everyday actions can make an impact.

New conceptual designs for products, architecture, and community development promote innovation and help us find new solutions. Starting with design contests, school projects, or in brainstorming sessions, these designs can help us reduce our environmental impact, become more resilient, and transform everyday life.

The arts bring us together and give us a form of exploration and expression, beyond our common state of mind. Sustainable art resonates with an emerging generation of artists who combine an aesthetic sensibility with a constructively critical approach to how we live, work, and interact with nature. These art forms can be motivated by ecology, politics, societal norms, and possibilities. They can celebrate nature and be used to educate, inspire, and inform us. The arts are one bridge towards a stronger connection with our natural environment and it is an avenue to find new solutions to environmental or societal issues.

The following are some project ideas for using art to promote environmental awareness in our communities:

- Host a design competition for an art installation that raises awareness about reducing waste.

- Host an art show with an environmental theme such as photography, painting, mixed media, sculpture, or other art forms.

- Use murals to bring images of the surrounding nature into the city.

- Organize a fund-raiser showcasing local culinary art for an environmental cause.

- Integrate environmental art projects or courses into existing art programs and schools.

- Host a class to make environmentally friendly paints and recycled canvas and frames.

- Find local waste sources and make it a classroom challenge to make a new product from the waste (e.g., grain bags turned into bean bag chairs for kid's lounge).

# 12
## *The Green Economy and Entrepreneurship*

As a student of biology throughout university, I knew business as "the bad guy." Destroying ecosystems, taking from nature without replenishing, all for the purpose of profit — that was the nature of business, I was taught. This discourse made me resent commerce and while in many scenarios this is justified, I have also seen businesses be an incredible force for positive change.

Our local economies are part of the fabric of our communities, providing jobs, well-being, and a sense of purpose. At a community level, green-economic strategies can have a triple-bottom-line benefit. Changing how we do business to reduce environmental impact relieves pressure on natural systems, taking special care of the people who work within our business, and the supply chain helps create strong and healthy communities. Shifting towards a green economy generates new streams of revenue with new business models, products, and services.

A green economy is an essential element of a green community. Engaging commerce in practices that reflect a triple bottom line can have a ripple effect that goes far beyond the walls of business. The green economy can generate new jobs, community wealth, and prosperity in the long term. It spans many sectors, including technology, hospitality, education, and agriculture. Shifting the way we live and work to reduce our environmental footprint and make our communities special, connected places is all part of this movement.

## 1. Local Economy

The hype about "local" is a full-scale North American movement to support our own communities. Initiatives to raise awareness about local buying are spearheaded by groups such as Buy Local BC, Local First Arizona, even national portals such as ShopLocal.us that all wave the local flag and encourage citizens to support businesses within and owned by their community.

Buying local means choosing locally made products, locally grown products, and shopping at locally owned stores. The scope of what is "local" depends on your perspective. It could be your town, region, or state or province. It could also refer to a national scale, supporting domestic goods and services.

You might ask why a local economy is so important. After all, globalization has given us great things such as international trade and an increase in national economic prosperity, job differentiation, and pineapples in the middle of the Canadian winter. So, really, what is so great about local?

Research is showing that there is a profound economic impact by keeping a higher percentage of money cycling within a defined community. It has been argued that strong local economies can withstand economic downturns better than those dependent on international markets, making communities more resilient. For every dollar that is spent with a locally owned company, a higher percentage stays in the community. This in turn creates more jobs, and more local spending. The result is a strong cyclical economy. A spin-off benefit is the innovation that community-based economies foster. With more money in the local community, businesses can take greater risks, open new concept restaurants, and be creative. New ideas become new businesses, which generates new revenue streams and attracts more entrepreneurs and investors.

A study by Sustainable Seattle on the local food economy suggests that locally directed spending by consumers more than doubles the number of dollars circulating among businesses and "locally directed buying and selling connects the community's resources to its needs resulting in relationships that serve to restore the land and regenerate community."[1]

Try to imagine a community without locally owned businesses. It would be very bland. Imagine, an entire box-store culture, without the boutique, iconic destinations that we know and love in a community. Thinking about your hometown, what are the iconic places that the community gathers in, and visitors come to see? Did they start as locally owned businesses? I bet many of them did. They add richness to the culture of our communities. They can become destinations, landmarks, and beacons for what our communities are all about.

One of my favorite examples is Captain Tony's Saloon in Key West, Florida. Over the decades this pub has been frequented by Ernest Hemingway and other well-known people. In its glory, you would often find Captain Tony himself working the bar. The place is covered in memorabilia from visitors and fans. To venture a guess at how many police badges are above the bar, I would say maybe 500. The place is an icon in Key West, and it has left behind a legacy that many try to emulate today.

Another great example was an experiment Portland launched in 2010 that would encourage and reward local shopping. They called the program "Supportland" and launched a digital card that would collect points for local buying. Supportland was created to build a mass of small, independent businesses and work together to engage the consumers. The program, which is referred to as "an airline-miles program on local-loving steroids," has been highly successful. So much so, that it is now launching in other cities, even outside of the US. The crew envisions the future of Supportland to consist of "mini-networks thriving all over the world with merits transferable among all locations."[2] Imagine traveling all over the world, using Supportland and its partners, to find the local hangouts. This may be the future of supporting local ownership.

In today's world, it is nearly impossible for any community to operate in complete economic isolation; however, building a local economy can earn self-reliance while strengthening community bonds, creating new jobs, and enhancing the culture and sense of place. When you pop into Joe's shoe repair, a local family owned business, it is likely that you will see a familiar face behind the counter,

---

1 "Why Local Linkages Matter: Findings from the Local Food Economy Study," Viki Sonntag, PhD, Sustainable Seattle, accessed March 2015. http://www.usask.ca/agriculture/plantsci/hort2020/local_linkages.pdf

2 "Our Story," Supportland, accessed February 2015. https://supportland.com/ourstory

and the dollars you spend at Joe's, he's probably going to spend it at the local pub or the local grocery store. The point is, the money stays in the community. Having a strong local component to an economy is not only a strategy for financial resilience, it can also be good for the environment. Inherently, local businesses are more connected to their community and the environment that surrounds it. Because of this proximity and awareness, they are more willing to change practices to reduce environmental impact.

The following are a few ideas to help your community do more to support the local commerce:

- Start a farmers' market if there isn't one already in your community. You can host specific markets for artisans, farmers, and more.

- Raise awareness about great local products and services with a local buying campaign.

- Create a consumer card for local shopping. The card, similar to the "Supportland" program, can collect points that are eligible for certain prizes.

- Encourage large purchasers, such as your local government, schools, and private corporations to shift their procurement practices and policies towards local providers.

- Start a community-supported agriculture (CSA) box program to make it easier for people to buy produce directly from farmers. CSA programs deliver a box of fresh produce on a regular basis to its members. These programs are great ways to connect the community to farm fresh produce and it helps secure regular buyers for farmers.

## 2. Green Business Practices

Any business can assess its environmental impact and find ways to reduce it. Often, business and industry are huge contributors to the total carbon footprint of a community. Sectors such as hospitality, transportation, and manufacturing require large amounts of energy to operate, and create high volumes of waste. It is important to engage these businesses and help them find ways to effectively reduce their environmental footprint.

There are a number of ways a community can work with the business sector to encourage green practices, but there are a few things to keep in mind. Businesses are in place to make a profit. Whether or not our personal ethics align with the fundamentals of capitalism, it is a reality and we must work with it to make change with existing business.

Reducing the environmental impact is something that my company, Synergy Enterprises, specializes in (www.synergyenterprises. ca). Synergy was founded to help businesses through the processes of going green. Diagram 5 shows the four distinct phases make up a successful sustainability program that will not only reduce environmental impact, but will also save costs and improve staff morale and customer loyalty.

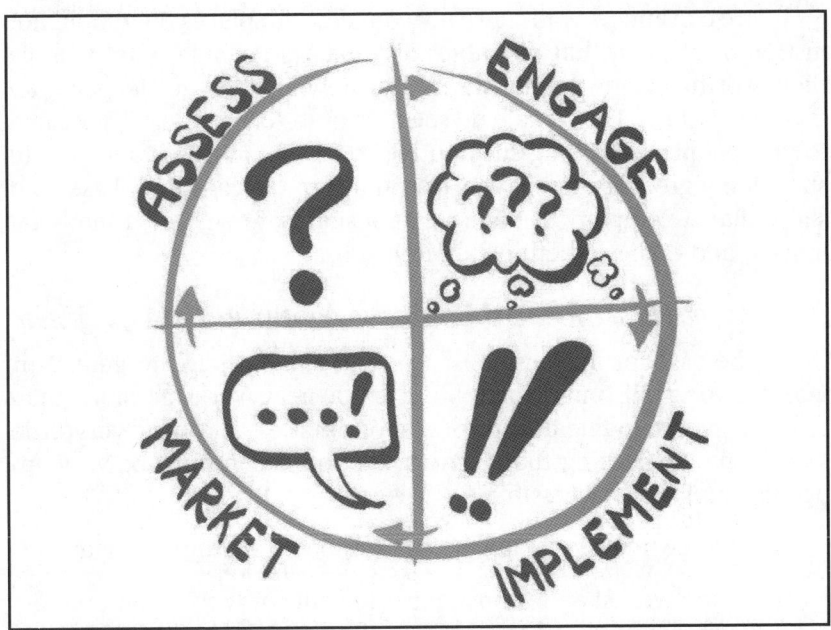

Diagram 5: Synergy's Four Stages of Sustainability

Many companies I have worked with are going green because they personally feel it is the right thing to do, and while ethics are their primary motive, they cannot compromise their bottom line completely. They still need to make payroll, pay their vendors, and invest in their infrastructure.

A stronger narrative, that really engages business, is one that focuses on both "what's in it for the planet" and "what's in it for the business." If a business can reduce costs, motivate employees, and become more attractive to customers, it is a no brainer for businesses to look at going green. In a survey Synergy conducted in 2012, it found that the number one driver for green business practices was ethics at the executive level — they truly wanted to be doing their part. However, the number one barrier to businesses going green was the perception of additional costs. Often, ethics are the driver that gets businesses engaged, but it is the cost savings that justify the changes.

Cost savings are gained through reduction of energy use, and water and gas consumption. Reducing wasted resources, moving to bulk packaging, reducing staff travel and shipping are also big cost savers. Perhaps more importantly, going green adds to the element of a brand; it adds to what it stands for.

More consumers want to really connect with places they shop, not just on price point, but on values. Companies nowadays must prove their worthiness to the consumer by showing they go deeper than the bottom line. This is called "social license to operate." They need to give people something substantial, some link to their value set. In sum, going green is a great way to connect to the consumer base, and show that a company is taking responsibility for its environmental impact, and doing something about it.

## 2.1 Encourage the local business community to go green

While the case for businesses is strong, it can be tough to gain their interest. After all, most small-business owners work far more than full-time hours, juggle dozens of responsibilities, and have very little spare time. Something that garners their attention must be very appealing, and easily accessible.

Here a few ideas to help get your business community engaged:

- Host a workshop for businesses to show how they can tangibly go green while reducing costs.

- Include a sustainability or environmental award in your local Chamber of Commerce or business club.

- Encourage the local government to offer incentives and rebates to businesses that switch to green practices.

- Educate the consumer about supporting green businesses.

- Encourage large buyers to include environmental criteria on their "request for proposal" process for suppliers, to encourage those bidding to showcase their green initiatives.

- Provide businesses with incentives and grants for green retrofits.

Localized certification programs are another way to get your business community engaged in green practices. Check out the programs in Maryland, San Francisco, Portland, Vancouver Island, and Austin. All of these cities have local green-business programs and certifications with localized criteria to encourage businesses to take action on environmental issues that are salient to that community and surrounding ecosystem. For example, water waste may be more of an issue in desert states than in coastal rainforest areas and energy consumption may be of greater concern in an area powered by coal generators than a community powered by a clean energy source. Though each criteria set is slightly different, the certifications offer a visible brand recognized by local residents.

There are also international green business certifications available, such as ISO 14001 and the Green Business Bureau. New certifications are emerging, such as B Corp, which focuses on triple-bottom-line business practices, adding criteria for social, community, and governance performance. To become a B Corp is relatively challenging, but many companies have said the process is incredibly rewarding. Certification programs such as these form clusters of like-minded companies. They often build a support network, giving each other business or even forming new businesses together.

### Table 3
### Examples of Green Business Programs and Criteria

| Program | Criteria |
| --- | --- |
| Vancouver Island Green Business Certification (VIGBC) | Retail, restaurant, and office-based businesses on Vancouver Island. |
| B Corp Certification | Companies of any size, great for consumer-facing businesses and large companies. |
| Dine Green | Great resource guide and criteria for food-based businesses, primarily in the US. |
| Green Business Bureau | Online certification for companies around the globe in a variety of sectors. |

## 3. New, Green Businesses and Jobs

The green economy is described as one that works to mitigate environmental issue through commerce. In the process of both greening existing companies and creating new, green companies, a new subsector is born within a community. This "green sector" includes services and products that generate rewarding jobs. While other jobs diminish due to changes in the economy, and the use of machines to replace people, the green economy helps a community flourish.

The green sector is innovative and collaborative — new partnerships and products are born to address environmental and social issues. Both the corporate and nonprofit worlds can benefit and work together in this space. Developing and nurturing this sector can strengthen the community and empower individuals to become entrepreneurs, or "ecopreneurs."

Table 4 shows a few, unique environmental ventures that have resulted in more jobs, and a healthier planet.

### Table 4
### Environmental Ventures

| Business Venture | Job Creation | Environmental Benefit |
|---|---|---|
| **Island Java Bag**<br><br>In partnership with Oughtred Coffee & Tea for the source of burlap.<br><br>www.javabag.ca | Two to three women making purses, bags, and growler carriers using burlap.<br><br>The jobs are flexible and given to women who need to be available for children with special needs. | The burlap is a waste product that comes from coffee roasters. Too fibrous to be composted through the commercial system, the burlap is up-cycled into new products that creates new jobs. |
| **Biophilia Design**<br><br>http://biophiliacollective.ca/ | A landscape architect and welder work together and with affiliates to design and build beautiful plant art installations such as living walls. | Bringing beautiful gardens to homes, corporations, and cities, Biophilia raises awareness about natural environments and brings green spaces to urban life. |
| **Farm to Baby**<br><br>http://farmtobabynyc.tumblr.com/ | Supports local farmers and creates jobs in packaging, marketing, and delivering the subscription orders. | Subscription-based baby-food delivery service in New York City. The company uses locally grown produce, picked just days before being gently cooked in its kitchen, to deliver fresh foods packaged in reusable glass containers. |

Vancouver, BC, has announced its intent to become "the greenest city in the world." This sparked some new research to discover the economic impact of a green city. The Vancouver Economic Commission CEO stated that the green economy has outpaced the broader economy in job growth. On a global level, studies have found that Corporate Social Responsibility (CSR) initiatives were not foregone during the recession in 2008. In fact, those efforts gained an upward swing after the recession.

It goes to say that sustainability is more than just recycling and reducing energy; it's about resilience in a holistic way. Preserving natural resources for future generations, creating jobs in a growing sector, increasing local spending — these are all things that result in stronger economies and societies. The web of impact from one action to another makes them inseparable.

The definition of a green job is an occupation that has a focus on those activities that restore or preserve environmental quality; reduce energy, materials, and water consumption; decarbonize the economy; and minimize or altogether avoid the generation of all forms of waste and pollution.

Key green economy sectors include:

- Local food and agriculture.

- Upcycling waste into new products.

- Recycling and composting services.

- Low- or zero-emission transportation options.

- Green services such as consulting, education, planning, and facilitation.

- Green building, construction, and trades.

- Green building products such as flooring and windows.

- Land remediation (e.g., water, soil).

- Carbon-reducing projects and green technologies.

- New business model development (e.g., hybrids, social venture).

## 3.1 Innovative business

Finding businesses with creative solutions to environmental issues is very exciting. The world of commerce can do incredible things, when motivated to make a difference. One of these inspiring businesses is Vittrium Building Products (www.vittrium.com). In homes, restaurants, hotels, and cafés, Vittrium has installed beautiful recycled glass countertops made from beer bottles, window glass, and liquor bottles. The materials are acquired from the local community and turned into fantastic new products. Here is a company that is creating new jobs and offering new, green-product options in a traditional sector. What's more, in the manufacturing process, Vittrium uses a gray-water system to re-catch and recycle water, drastically reducing the water that would be needed.

# 13
# *Sustainable Cities and Helping Yours Become One*

 In North America, while sporadic federal, state, and provincial steps have been taken on climate change over the years, action on sustainability has been most consistently and prominently led by cities and communities. Many of these programs have come and gone, but commitments at the community level tend to be more resilient to political change and once they take hold in a community, they tend to stay. This is good news for you and the engaged citizens who are looking to make things happen. By connecting with your local government representatives, you can help lead and support changes in your community that not only last but could also spread across to other communities. Local governments work together and watch each other for new ideas. These ideas are willingly shared across communities, as the likelihood of success increases when other cities adopt policies and implement new sustainable solutions. Talking to your local authority about your ideas for change can lead to big things.

# 1. Cities That Lead

Why reinvent the wheel? Learn from the many cities who have been working at resolving sustainability challenges for years. Which cities are the greenest cities? There is a group that are consistent leaders in North America for sustainability rankings. No need for us to rank them, but consider the cities in this chapter to be the leading examples.

Thirty years ago, North American cities were not even in the discussions for "greenest city in the world" nominations. European cities were far ahead in energy, transportation, waste management, and every other facet you can think of. Now the West Coast is seen as a world leader in sustainability, but there are cities across the US and Canada that are leading in different ways.

There are many sustainability ratings for green cities that use a range of metrics and indicators. Some argue that livability rankings are even more important because they provide a better balance of social and equity measures. What we provide in the following sections, in no particular order, are six North American cities that we feel are consistently included at the top of green-rating systems. These cities have taken steps that truly make them leaders that other cities should observe and will show some opportunities that you can consider championing in your community.

All of these great green cities have one common thread, leadership. Establishing a vision for sustainability at the highest level of any organization sets the tone for everything else, in this case, the community. This kind of leadership forces the entire organization to look at how it functions and to ask how it could operate in a more sustainable manor. Making sustainability a part of regular municipal business will eventually pay off because a sustainable city will become an efficient and well-planned city. When a city's workers begin thinking about sustainability, they consider the longer term and the beneficiaries within the community. With this lens, investments in the city make them more efficient and effective in the future. For example, energy-efficient buildings should be mandatory for every municipality and something that is demanded by taxpayers. Municipal buildings will always be taxpayer properties and short-sighted investment in infrastructure will only come back to haunt the tax payer.

This is a significant concern all across North America, but particularly in the US, where the cost of avoiding the repairs to deteriorating infrastructure and roads is being realized. This may seem to some as looking at an issue outside of sustainability, but it has everything to do with building and supporting a green community. When finances run short, attention to sustainability and long-term thinking tends to fall short as well. Fiscal responsibility sets the stage for a mayor to act on sustainability, but as most of these cities know, these two ideals need to work side by side to be successful.

## 1.1 Vancouver

This city of Vancouver, British Columbia, regularly gets the top nod in global sustainability rankings these days and justifiably so. Setting a goal to be the greenest city in the world has set a tone across the city and it is pushing the boundaries of sustainability on all fronts. It's gets specific recognition for the ambitious goal of carbon-neutral buildings by 2020 and aims to transform its transportation systems to greatly increase transit and cycling options throughout the city.[1]

## 1.2 San Francisco

San Francisco, California, is a dense city of 837,442 people, which lends itself to energy and transportation efficiency. A report by Siemens attributes its sustainability performance to connecting private companies with pioneering green initiatives such as energy-awareness programs and green transportation.[2] The city is also known for its incredible 77 percent recycling rate, one of the best in the world, made possible through city directives calling for separation of recyclable and compostable materials from landfill waste.

## 1.3 Portland

The city of Portland, Oregon, is a unique example of a sustainable city; so unique that you could base a show on its oddities (and someone did: *Portlandia*). What could be perceived as a quirky, eccentric attitude to environmental and social welfare is really a serious commitment to community-based sustainability. Portland is one of the leading cities in utilizing renewable energy sources, which represent 33 percent of its total energy demand. The US national average is 13 percent.[3]

## 1.4 Seattle

Seattle, Washington, has been a green leader for a long time, but new energy benchmarking requirements for buildings are pushing all

1 "Vancouver the Greenest City in Canada, Index Shows," *The Globe and Mail*, accessed February 2015. http://www.theglobeandmail.com/news/british-columbia/vancouver-the-greenest-city-in-canada-index-shows/article4183673/
2 "San Francisco Green City Rate," Siemens, accessed February 2015. http://www.siemens.com/entry/cc/en/greencityindex.htm
3 "Get to Know the Top Ten Greenest Cities in the World for 2014," Green Uptown, accessed February 2015. http://www.greenuptown.com/get-to-know-the-top-ten-greenest-cities-in-the-world-for-2014/

new developments to the highest level of energy performance in the county. Early adoption of Leadership in Energy and Environmental Design (LEED) certification requirements for municipal buildings set an early tone in the local building community. Seattle has also set a goal to be a carbon neutral city by 2050.

## 1.5 Toronto

Toronto, Ontario, is the largest city in Canada, and the fourth largest in North America. It has the energy challenge of dealing with cold winters and humid summers. Toronto has shown a balanced approach to sustainability performance across all categories, but in particular waste reduction and energy and emissions reductions. Toronto was also the first city in North America to introduce a bylaw to require the construction of green roofs on all new developments.

## 1.6 New York

Hurricane Sandy was a wakeup call for many inhabitants of New York, the largest city in the US, as well as many other inhabitants on the eastern seaboard. A taste of the potential impacts from global warming brought climate change adaptation discussion to the forefront, resulting in the PlaNYC effort. This plan sought to address the long-term challenges that could affect the city's economy and aging infrastructure by integrating initiatives and milestones throughout the many city agencies.

However, the city had been working on sustainability initiatives long before the hurricane, providing strong leadership on carbon reductions, water- and air-quality initiatives, and transportation challenges. In one of the boldest transportation changes made in North America, New York transformed one of the busiest downtown core vehicle arteries into a cycling and pedestrian haven. People have found that new protected bike lanes are actually speeding up vehicle traffic in a town that was legendary for its traffic jams up to only ten years ago.

## 1.7 International cities worth watching

If you are looking for international inspiration, research the cities listed below as they are considered the world's greenest. If it can work in Copenhagen, why not where you live? These cities started years ahead of North American cities, and they have some amazing feats of sustainability that can inspire actions in our own communities. The kind of feats we are talking about include 50 percent of energy demand met by solar energy in Germany and 50 percent cycling participation in Denmark.

Here is a list of international cities that are worth investigating further if you want to see where our sustainable steps today may eventually lead:

- Copenhagen, Denmark.
- Oslo, Norway.
- Freiburg, Germany.
- Stockholm, Sweden.
- Vienna, Austria.
- Cape Town, South Africa.
- Curitiba, Brazil.
- Singapore, Singapore.
- Adelaide, Australia.
- London, England.
- Bogotá, Colombia.

## 2. What Makes a Community a Green Leader?

What is it about sustainable cities that make them unique and what are the factors that lead to their success? The history, geography, and culture of a city can greatly influence the opportunity for a sustainable city to emerge, but there are some key factors that helped make the above list of cities become what they are today.

### 2.1 Green champions

There are many city planners and engineers who have helped champion change in communities. However, often it is the mayors of these cities who have the greatest power and influence to champion green changes in a community because of their strong interface with many stakeholder groups such as chambers of commerce, politicians, community members, nonprofits, government agencies, and more.

London's Mayor Boris Johnson is a cycling enthusiast which led him to start "Leading to a Greener London." This initiative included commitments to increase the number of low-emission vehicles in the city. An ambitious goal of 100,000 electric vehicles (EV) by 2015 was set which would be support by 25,000 new EV charging stations.

Vancouver's Mayor Gregor Robertson has experienced many battles with the development community through one of the biggest real estate and property value booms the world has seen. Yet he and his council has held firm to sustainability commitments including controversial cycling lane construction in the tight downtown core and in well-established suburbs and Leadership in Energy and Environmental Design (LEED) requirements for all new buildings in the city.

Enrique Peñalosa, former mayor of Bogota, Columbia, is profiled in Charles Montgomery's excellent book, *Happy City*. Peñalosa changed the city, by focusing on people by prioritizing parks and public spaces, and valuing the bicycle as much as the car. His changes were not popular with everyone, and he did not win the next election, but he is credited with improving the mobility of the city by using strong measures to discourage private vehicle use.

The following are some common traits of green cities and their leaders:

- Commitments are imbedded in community policy and important documents such as official community plans.

- Creators of high-profile projects that send a signal of commitment. Transportation or building projects that raise the sustainability bar in a community.

- Risk takers and not afraid to make decisions that will not please everyone. These leaders know that people are much more adaptable than they first appear to be.

- They develop smart transportation and energy policies that are integrated and enforced in their communities.

- Communicate clear messages and remember that it's about the people. (**Note:** If sustainability is not presented to people in a way that everyone can understand, you will find yourself alone in your battle.)

---

### Small Programs can lead to Big Changes:
### Tap by Tap Showerhead Exchange Program

Sometimes an idea whose time has seemed to have already passed needs to be revisited. Low-flow showerheads would normally draw eye-rolls because they were seen as ineffective. However, when a green building nonprofit identified an improvement in technology and a potential benefit to multiple partners, an effective project was piloted.

In 2011, the Tap by Tap program was piloted by City Green Solutions in Saanich, British Columbia. The program was designed to engage local residents in simple cost-, energy-, and water-saving actions, by installing high-efficiency showerheads and faucet aerators. Simply put, efficient showerheads were given to residents if they returned their old ones. More than 1,000 residents participated in the program and the community benefited from reduced greenhouse gas emissions and less strain on natural water sources. By installing an energy-saving and a water-saving kit, they cumulatively saved more than 40,000 liters of water each year and saved $70 to $135 on energy bills each year per home.

---

## 3. Working with City Hall

Let's say you find an interesting green idea for your community on the web and you want to find out if it is possible to bring this idea to your community. If you aren't familiar with ways to communicate with your city or local government, it can be daunting trying to figure out who is the right person to talk to.

If you are looking for some advice about getting someone's attention at city hall, we suggest being polite but persistent. Government and taxpayer interactions can be often described as "unsustainable" to be sure, but this is a permanent partnership. City employees are just like you, they are looking to be treated with respect, and they are more likely to assist you with your new idea if you approach it with a positive focus.

By persistent, we mean don't let one government employee put you off your idea. Apply slow, steady pressure. People hate being pushed into things, so work with them and let them become a part of the solution. You have a goal is mind, but you have to be open to the route that you take to get there. Also keep in mind that the employee you may think is responsible might not really have the ability or the authority to consider your changes so try to find someone who does!

You may have heard about the comparison between managers and leaders before? You may need to find a leader in the community and that doesn't necessarily mean the top of the organizational chart. Find someone who has already led change in the community and who is familiar with the change process. Perhaps this isn't someone who works for the city, but a community association representative or non-profit champion who knows where the path for success lies. A little planning could help bring your idea to life.

Commitments are imbedded in the community goals, and if they aren't, they need to be! People need to be able to point to a commitment that is made, so that they feel their community has their back. Integrate commitments into official community plans or within separate sustainability plans (e.g., climate action, urban forest).

What is important to your community? Can you align your project with the existing commitments the city holds? Clean air and a healthy environment are commitments that many communities have made, and sustainability initiatives such as green energy and electric vehicles strongly support these more established commitments.

You can also suggest to your local government that it provides free or low-cost permits to support green buildings and green-energy installations. These are generally lower costs that likely won't shift a home owner's purchasing decision, but it will show a community commitment to action. For example, free permits for solar installations are a small but committed step to encouraging uptake.

Governments have often used tax credits as incentives to boost sustainability in a specific area. Subject to the government level, tax credits and incentives are used to encourage community revitalization, retain city residents, and reduce development costs. In the US, federal tax credits have been used to increase sustainability projects and have assisted the development of green low-income housing projects and the preservation of public facilities.

# 14
# *Measure Success*

No matter the scale of your project, it is valuable to measure and monitor the results. The performance metrics or key performance indicators (KPIs) that you use should reflect the values and purpose of the project. For example, when greening a business, the success should be measured in a triple bottom line, with KPIs for social, economic, and environment. Often when I speak of KPIs, I'm met with eye rolls and yawns, but don't get bored yet — measuring success and seeing the results can be very rewarding.

## 1. Measuring at the Project Level

At the outset of your project, utilize the SMART principles[1] to set achievable goals and targets. SMART goals focus a group and keep the target clear. This can make a group more efficient, and everyone will understand where progress is at relevant to the goal. Using a simple system like this removes confusion and helps people focus on the objective at hand.

Let's use Table 5 as an example of a project to clean up a river system.

---

1 "There's a S.M.A.R.T. Way to Write Management's Goals and Objectives," George T. Doran *Management Review*, AMA Forum, 1981.

## Table 5
## River Cleanup Project SMART Goals

| | |
|---|---|
| Specific:<br>*Target a specific area for improvement.* | Reduce water toxicity levels by 50 percent, and trash debris from the river ways by 90 percent, educating industry about contaminants, arranging waterway cleanup crews, putting up "no polluting" signage and providing trash receptacles. In addition, there will be a general awareness campaign. |
| Measureable:<br>*Have an indicator for progress.* | Water-toxicity levels will be measured quarterly throughout the year to determine success. In addition, scan of the shoreline, count the debris, and measure how much it is being reduced. We will also measure success of our outreach via social media, press, and newsletter. |
| Achievable:<br>*Specify goals that are reachable.* | With dedicated effort, and drawing on partnerships and the local community, it is possible to reach these goals in 12 months or less. |
| Realistic:<br>*These goals are attainable with the available resources.* | The funding for the toxicity-level testing has been secured. We have the volunteer and staff capacity to complete these tasks. |
| Time:<br>*The goals have specific time frames.* | This project will occur in stages over the next 12 months with quarterly meetings to determine progress and the next steps. |

For my company, Synergy, we have annual KPIs in three categories:

- **Social:** We set volunteer hours for community groups, and aim to do a certain level of skill training and professional development with our staff.

- **Environmental:** We set goals to reduce carbon emissions, energy consumption, and waste.

- **Economic:** We set revenue and profit goals for the year.

All of these combined set our direction and help us measure progress as we move through the year. It keeps everyone focused in an environment where it is easy to get distracted and stray from the task with the next new shiny project.

Setting goals is one thing and many groups do that part. Measuring progress over time is something not all groups do as well. To make sure the goals become enacted, make them visual, share them through an online forum, and post them in an office. Make sure it is someone's job to track progress towards those goals and report to other stakeholders. See Table 6 for an example.

## 2. Measuring at the City Level

An entire city can measure its sustainability rating including factors for people, planet, and prosperity categories using the STAR Community Rating System[2] developed by a collaboration of experts and organizations focusing on community-level sustainability. The STAR framework recognizes sustainable communities and provides a measure to benchmark performance and plan for improvements and set targets along the way. The first cities to achieve the Five Stars, the highest level of certification, were Northampton, Massachusetts; and Seattle, Washington.

A community can use this rating system, or a similar model with multiple indicators, as a reference for official community plans. When a city benchmarks performance and reports to its citizens, it keeps a pulse-check on how the community is doing overall and how things are shifting year to year.

Engaged citizens, like yourself, can shape your community and our future as a global society. Advocates, leaders, facilitators, and change-makers have introduced new ideas, projects, and innovations into our communities for generations. Now, more than ever, we need leaders and engaged citizens to tackle problems small and large. Collectively, we can make our communities great, and create a sustainable, prosperous future for generations to come.

---

2 STAR Community Rating System, accessed February 2015.
https://reporting.starcommunities.org/communities.

## Table 6
## Key Performance Indicators:
## Local Business Example

| Social | Environment | Economic |
|---|---|---|
| • Staff community volunteer time.<br>• Percentage of employees making a living wage.<br>• Annual donations.<br>• Professional development and educational investment in staff.<br>• Hiring people with special needs. | • Recycling performance (diversion rate).<br>• Total energy and water usage and savings.<br>• Carbon footprint compared to baseline year.<br>• Number of staff who bike, walk, or take transit to work. | • Gross revenue.<br>• Revenue growth rate over time.<br>• Profit margins.<br>• Average order value.<br>• Operating expenses as a percentage of total expenses.<br>• Customer retention rate. |
| **Tracking:**<br>• Accounting system.<br>• Staff time-tracking sheets. | **Tracking:**<br>• Annual environmental audit.<br>• Staff commuting survey. | **Tracking:**<br>• Customer relationship management tool.<br>• Accounting system. |